Filmguide to

Triumph of the Will

RICHARD MERAN BARSAM

INDIANA UNIVERSITY PRESS
Bloomington   London

Published in Canada by Fitzhenry & Whiteside Limited, Don Mills, Ontario
Manufactured in the United States of America

Library of Congress Cataloging in Publication Data
Barsam, Richard Meran.
  Filmguide to Triumph of the will.
  (Indiana University Press filmguide series)
  Bibliography
  1. Triumph of the will [Motion picture]
2. Nationalsozialistische Deutsche Arbeiter-Partei
Reichsparteitag. 6th, Nuremberg, 1934. I. Title.
II. Series.
DD253.28 1934.B37   791.43'7   74-6517
ISBN 0-253-39319-1 cl.
ISBN 0-253-39320-5 pbk.

Filmguide to

Triumph of the Will

INDIANA UNIVERSITY PRESS FILMGUIDE SERIES
Harry M. Geduld and Ronald Gottesman,
General Editors

FOR JENNIFER

contents

preface

This little book could hardly have been written without the diversified help of many people whom I should like to thank here: Renata von Stoephasius, who translated the German speeches and assisted in preparing the final manuscript; Jonas Mekas and P. Adams Sitney, who gave me access to material on Leni Riefenstahl before they published it in *Film Culture* (Spring 1973); Margareta Akermark and Charles Silver of the Museum of Modern Art, who arranged countless screenings for me; Gerald Mast, who generously read and criticized my manuscript and whose expert counsel was of great help; Walter A. Verbanic, who provided me with his translation of *Hinter den Kulissen des Reichsparteitagfilms;* Kathleen Endress Kasper, who prepared much preliminary material and the bibliography; Harry M. Geduld and Ronald Gottesman, for their support; and Mark Berman, for his encouragement.

Further, I wish to thank the Research Foundation of the City University of New York for a generous grant which made it possible for me to visit Germany and Austria in preparation for this study.

Finally, I record my gratitude to Leni Riefenstahl herself, who cooperated in many hours of interviews, opened her archive to my research, and took a genuine interest in this book. Also in Munich, my thanks to Horst Kettner and to Heinz Herzer.

RICHARD MERAN BARSAM

Filmguide to

Triumph of the Will

credits*

TRIUMPH OF THE WILL

Film of the NSDAP Party Rally

Commissioned by	National Socialist German Workers' Party
Producer	Leni Riefenstahl Studio—Film
Overall Direction and Artistic Production	Leni Riefenstahl
Photographic Direction	Sepp Allgeier
Music	Herbert Windt
Head Cameraman	Arthur Kiekebusch
Cameramen	Sepp Allgeier, Karl Attenberger, Werner Bohne, Walter Frentz, Hans Gottschalk, Werner Hundhausen, Herbert Kebelmann, Albert Kling, Franz Koch, Herbert Kutschbach, Paul Lieberenz, Richard Nickel,

* Note: the only credits to appear in the film itself are listed in the outline which follows.

	Walter Riml, Arthur von Schwert-führer, Karl Vass, Franz Weihmayr, Siegfried Weinmann, Karl Wellert
Camera Assistants	Sepp Ketterer, Wolf Hart, Peter Haller, Kurt Schulz, Eugen O. Bernhard, Richard Kandler, Hans Bühring, Richard Böhm, Erich Stoll, Josef Koch, Otto Jäger, August Beis, Hans Wittmann, Wolfgang Müller, Heinz Linke, Erich Küchler, Wilhelm Schmidt, Ernst Kunstmann, Erich Grohmann
Photography Workshop	Svend Nolan, Fritz Bunsch, Hans Noack
Aerial Photography	From the airship D/PN 30 (Captain Rolf Hanasch) and a Klemm aircraft (Pilot Anton Riediger, camera operated by Albert Kling)
Participating Newsreel Companies	Ufa, Duelig, Tobis-Melo, Fox, and Paramount
Sound Recordings and Sound System	Tobis-Klangfilm
Sound Engineer	Siefried Schulz
Assistant	Ernst Schütz
Sound Assistants	H. Bullerjahn, H. Degner, K. Drews, E. Eisenbach, H. Honicka, C. Kühns, E. Kropf, H. Loos, J. Richter, W. Rosskopf
Sound Editors	Bruno Hartwich, Alice Ludwig

Music Dubbing	Band of the SS Bodyguard Regiment (Adolf Hitler) under the direction of conductor Müller-John
Lighting	Bernhard Delschaft, Jr., of Koerting and Mathiesen A.G. in cooperation with Bernhard Delschaft, Sr., Felix Koziolek, Han Kubisch, Otto Schroeder, R. Bude, H. Compart, E. Erdmann, W. Fried, K. H. Grohwald, O. Hilbert, R. Radtke, F. Reinke, F. Rusch, K. Schreiber, W. Stangenberg
Still Photography	Rolf Lantin
Photography Enlargement and Editing	Gisela Lindeck-Schneeberger
Camera Installations	City Councilman Brugmann and Architect Seegy
Architect	Albert Speer
Propaganda Consultant, NSDAP	Herbert Seehofer
Local Arrangements in Nuremberg	Chief Councilman Gutterer and Councilmen Dürr, Wollner, and Bäselsöder
Business Managers	Walter Traut and Walter Groskopf
Assistants	Erna Peters, Guzzi and Otto Lantschner, Walter Prager
Volunteer	Wolfgang Brüning
Distributor	Ufa-Filmverleih G.m.b.H.
Release Date	March 28, 1935
Time	107 minutes

outline

Triumph of the Will

1. SCENE 1: Arrival in Nuremberg (10:30 mins.)
    A. Main titles, in four separate shots, here in English translation.
        1. *Triumph of the Will*
        2. The Documentary Film of the Reich's Party Congress 1934
        3. Produced by Orders of the *Führer*
        4. Created by Leni Riefenstahl
    B. Historical background, in four rolling titles, in four separate shots, here in English translation.
        1. On September 5, 1934, 20 years after the outbreak of the world war
        2. 16 years after the beginning of our suffering
        3. 19 months after the beginning of the German renaissance
        4. Adolf Hitler flew to Nuremberg again to review the columns of his faithful followers
    C. The *Führer's* flight to Nuremberg
    D. Motorcade from airport to city
    E. Arrival at hotel

2. SCENE 2: Band Concert and Rally (2:54 mins.)
    A. Hitler reviews band concert and rally outside hotel

3. SCENE 3: Nuremberg at Sleep, Play, and Work (10:27 mins.)
    A. The sleeping city

   B. The tent city of soldiers and workers
   C. The folk parade
   D. Troop review

4. SCENE 4: First Party Congress (9:30 mins.)
   A. Greeting of delegates by Rudolf Hess
   B. Remarks by 12 Nazi Party leaders

5. SCENE 5: Labor Service Rally (7:03 mins.)
   A. Konstantin Hierl introduces Hitler
   B. Labor Service ceremony of loyalty
   C. Hitler addresses workers

6. SCENE 6: Storm Troopers Rally (3:36 mins.)
   A. Viktor Lutze addresses storm troopers
   B. Fireworks display

7. SCENE 7: Youth Rally (10:04 mins.)
   A. Entrance of Hitler and party officials
   B. Address by Baldur von Schirach
   C. Address by Hitler
   D. Hitler's review of youth groups and departure

8. SCENE 8: Military and Cavalry Review (1:28 mins.)
   A. Hitler and military officials review display of military, artillery, and cavalry

9. SCENE 9: Twilight Rally (8:14 mins.)
   A. Twilight parade of flag bearers
   B. Hitler's address to assembled troops
   C. Parade of flags, banners, standards

10. SCENE 10: Tribute to War Dead (11:17 mins.)
   A. Hitler, Lutze, and Himmler pay tribute at war memorial
   B. Hitler reviews parade of storm troopers

    C. Lutze and Hitler address the storm troopers

    D. Consecration of flags ceremony

11. SCENE 11: Military Parade (18:04 mins.)

    A. Hitler and military and party officials review lengthy parade of troops leaving Nuremberg

12. SCENE 12: Closing Party Congress (15:10 mins.)

    A. Entrance of party officials and standard bearers

    B. Hitler's address to congress

    C. Hess' closing remarks

    D. Marching soldiers

    E. Closing titles, here in English translation

        1. *Triumph of the Will*

        2. The End

the director

Leni Riefenstahl and the
Burden of Independence

From her earliest years, Leni Riefenstahl dreamed of dancing or acting out her fantasies on the stage; in the role of Junta, the idealistic heroine of *The Blue Light* (1932), she fulfilled her dream. Riefenstahl was critically praised for writing, producing, and directing the film, but her real fulfillment came from playing the role of the young woman who has no contact with the real world and who is, therefore, destroyed by it. This unhappy story expresses Riefenstahl's belief that the artist must, at all costs, remain independent of the material world. In her own life, she has achieved artistic freedom, but at a great cost. Like Junta, she had her own intuitive feelings about nature and was destroyed by her naive disregard of the real world around her, the world she set out to avoid.

Bertha Helene (Leni) Amalie Riefenstahl was born on August 22, 1902, in Berlin. As a young woman, she studied painting, but her first love was modern dance and ballet. She created her own dances, for herself alone, and even designed her own costumes; her talent was recognized by the great German theater director Max Reinhardt, who engaged her as a dancer. By the age of twenty-four, she had given solo dance concerts in many European cities, but a knee injury forced her to stop dancing and to think about the future. While she was convalescing, she saw her first "mountain film" and was impressed by its beauty and by the beauty of the sports portrayed in it. (The mountain films are realistic adventure stories set in the Alps, but the stories are used only as a backdrop to show the physical and spiritual exhilaration that comes with the mastery of skiing and climbing. The striking and perhaps most memorable aspect of the mountain films is their reality: real snow, real ice, and real danger.) When Reinhardt asked her to play the heroine in his stage production of the German romantic tragedy *Penthesilea,* Riefenstahl was obliged to choose between his offer to make her stage debut as an actress and the offer of Arnold Fanck to make her film debut in one of his mountain films. She chose the film role, a decision that was to change her life.

Fanck stressed realism and usually hired winter sports experts rather than actors, but Riefenstahl proved to be as good an athlete as she had been a dancer, and starred in five of his films: *The Holy Mountain (Der Heilige Berg,* 1926); *The Great Leap (Der Grosse Sprung,* 1927); *The White Hell of Pitz Palu (Die Weisse Hölle von Piz Palü,* 1929, co-directed with G. W. Pabst); *Storm Over Mont Blanc (Stürme über dem Montblanc,* 1930, also known as *Avalanche); The White Frenzy (Der Weisse Rausch,* 1931); and *S.O.S. Iceberg (SOS Eisberg,* 1933; the American version was co-directed with Tay Garnett). In addition to the five films for Fanck, Riefenstahl was also featured in Rudolf Raffé's *The Fate of the von Haspburgs (Das Schicksal derer von Habsburg,* 1929).

The mountain films influenced the photographic style and, to a certain extent, the themes of Riefenstahl's two great nonfiction films: *Triumph of the Will (Triumph des Willens,* 1935) and *Olympia (Olympia,* 1938). The essence of mountain films is the contrast of the physical with the spiritual; the same controlling concept gives her own films a thematic consistency but, more important, infuses them with a cinematic tension that is so often lacking in other nonfiction films.

In 1931, Leni Riefenstahl established her own film production company; her first effort was *The Blue Light* (*Das Blaue Licht,* 1932). To the realistic mountain story, which she wrote with Béla Balázs, the noted Hungarian film writer, she added her own masterful sense of camera positioning and photography and her gift for editing. Riefenstahl's powerfully romantic imagination transformed the entertainment melodrama of the mountain film into a poetic statement. While 1932 marked the beginning of her independent film making career, it also marked the low point of the German economic depression. In an attempt to win power, Hitler claimed that the election of his National Socialist Party would create employment and prosperity for Germany. Riefenstahl believed these claims, and before January 1933, when Hitler became Chancellor, she met with him several times. She says that she was flattered by his praise for *The Blue Light,* but fearful of the influence he might have on her art. Her fears proved to be well-founded.

Hitler's rise to power in January 1933, began a new period of prosperity, but it also marked, among the other vast changes that were to affect German society, the end of the independent filmmaking industry as it was then known. Paul Joseph Goebbels, the Minister of Propaganda, took charge of every phase of filmmaking, including production, distribution, and research in technical matters; his first priority was the production of propaganda films. Leni Riefenstahl had the apparent choice of leaving Germany, as so many great artists and intellectuals did, or remaining to continue her career. She chose to stay, but her reasons are not clear. Perhaps she was an opportunist who wanted to capitalize on Hitler's admiration of her work; perhaps she was a patriot who believed that a German renaissance was imminent; or perhaps she was an idealistic young woman who believed that she could create her art free from the realities of the German social condition at that time.

The answer lies somewhere in a combination of such explanations. Riefenstahl readily admits that she was fascinated by Hitler's hypnotic power over people, but except for *Victory of Faith*—a lost film about which more will be said below—she did not join the Nazi party and she did not make films for it. Her films were made in her own production company and registered in her name. There is factual evidence that she was never a Nazi, although she is still thought by many to have been. In two denazification proceedings, in 1948 and 1952, West German courts held that she had been a "mere follower" of the party; like Junta in *The Blue Light,* she followed her beliefs, and like Junta, she was wrong.

Riefenstahl claims Arnold Fanck as her teacher and master, and his influence is apparent in the narrative and psychological aspects of her films, but her vivid sense of photography comes from the wider German tradition and her brilliant control of montage comes from the Russian tradition, especially from Eisenstein. Riefenstahl says that she was familiar with the work of her predecessors and that she was very impressed by Eisenstein's *Potemkin* (1925) and, to a lesser extent, by Abel Gance's *Napoleon* (1927). But there is an obvious difference in their approaches to documentary: *Potemkin* and *Napoleon* record history staged for the cameras, while *Triumph of the Will* records history as it happened. Indeed, in the matter of influence, Riefenstahl claims never to have heard of John Grierson, the founder of the British documentary film school in the 1930s, until he came to her defense against British criticism in the 1960s. She responds to the names of other great nonfiction filmmakers—Robert Flaherty, Joris Ivens, and Pare Lorentz—with only faint recognition. It seems clear that Riefenstahl founded and carried on her own tradition.

In *The Blue Light,* Hitler recognized Riefenstahl's talent to transfer an abstract ideal to the screen and, at the same time, to infuse it with dramatic realism. But Hitler's choice of her to make a film of the 1933 party rally was the source of a bitter confrontation between him and Goebbels because Goebbels wanted to make all decisions regarding Nazi film production. In August 1933, a few days before the fifth party rally was to begin in Nuremberg, Hitler summoned Riefenstahl and asked about her preparations for the rally film, the first time, she says, that she had heard anything about the project. She says Hitler was very upset because Goebbels had apparently boycotted his order and not informed her about the film. She feels that Goebbels was prejudiced against her lack of political commitment, against her age (she was 31), against her inexperience as a filmmaker, and against her as a woman. Without Goebbels' assistance in Nuremberg, she shot several thousand feet of film. Although she was dissatisfied with the footage, Hitler ordered that it be edited and released (on December 1, 1933) as *Victory of Faith (Sieg des Glaubens)*. The film was produced by the Nazi party, but unfortunately all prints of it seem to have been lost or destroyed; Riefenstahl asserts that her name did not appear in the credits. Determined never to be put in such a situation again, Riefenstahl told Hitler of the obstacles she had encountered. She says that he was angry over Goebbels' interference and ordered her to make the film of the 1934 rally—*Triumph of the Will*.

Because she had never made a nonfiction film, she sought the help of her friend Walter Ruttmann, the director of the famous German documentary *Berlin: The Symphony of a Great City* (1927). She says that he was enthusiastic, especially to create a film prologue showing the Nazi rise to power. With the financial backing of Ufa, the German film collective, an agreement was reached that the 1934 party film would be produced by her independent company, Leni Riefenstahl Studio-Film. If the project had been completed as these discussions suggest, the film would have begun with Ruttmann's prologue and ended with Riefenstahl's rally footage; with this understanding, she left for Spain to prepare *Tiefland,* a film that she finally completed in 1954.

At the time, in the spring of 1934, the Nazi party was consolidating its power under Hitler even though it had become the ruling power in 1933. When President Paul von Hindenburg saw that he could no longer retain control of the nation, he appointed Adolf Hitler as Chancellor on January 30, 1933. The so-called "enabling act" of March 23, 1933, gave Hitler dictatorial powers. The German cabinet adopted a decree which would unite the offices of President and Chancellor on the occasion of the ailing von Hindenburg's death; thus, on August 2, 1934, Hitler became *Führer* of the Third Reich. One month later, he presided over the sixth party rally held in Nuremberg from September 4 to 10; *Triumph of the Will* is the film record of that gigantic display of party power.

In the middle of August, two weeks before the rally, Riefenstahl returned to Germany from Spain and realized that she would have to make the entire rally film. Ruttmann's footage was unacceptable to her; moreover, Rudolf Hess, Hitler's deputy, reminded her that Hitler had ordered her, not Ruttmann, to make the film. She attempted to persuade Hitler to change his mind, but he stood firm on his original order. When she complained to Hitler that she could not stand the interference of Goebbels' staff, Hitler reassured her that she would receive complete cooperation. When she told him that she had no conception of how to film parades and speeches, he responded that he had chosen her because she was an artist capable of the task. She protested that she did not know who or what was politically important, and quotes Hitler as responding: "It is not important who is in the film. It is important that the film has the atmosphere."[1] When she insisted again that she was not the right person for the task, she says that Hitler answered: "You are so young. Give me only six days of your life." She complained that it might require a year for her to edit the film, and that this would interfere with her *Tiefland* project. She says that Hitler listened to all of her objections, but asked that she undertake the rally film as a "personal favor" to him.

Realizing that Hitler would not change his mind, Riefenstahl listed the three conditions on which she would make the film, although it appears that she had little choice in the matter and that her conditions were another futile gesture toward independence. First, she insisted on freedom from Nazi party influence in financial, political, and aesthetic matters related to production. Second, she demanded complete authority over the final cut of the film. Third, she asked Hitler to promise that she would never have to make another film for the government, and that she could resume her own projects once the rally film was completed. She says that Hitler readily agreed to the conditions; however, he broke his promise to her on the final point. When *Triumph of the Will* was released, General Werner von Blomberg, Commander in Chief of the Army, complained to Hitler that Riefenstahl had neglected the importance of the German Army in the film; to satisfy the military, she was asked to make *Day of Freedom—Our Armed Forces* (*Tag der Freiheit—Unsere Wehrmacht,* 1935). This beautifully photographed and edited film vaguely resembles *Triumph of the Will,* but it is little more than a skillful assemblage of factual footage and lacks any of the thematic or psychological interest of its famous predecessor. The titles give credit to Riefenstahl as the director of production; with *Triumph of the Will,* the film was produced for the Nazi party by her own company.

After her discussion with Hitler, and confident that she was working on her own terms, Riefenstahl began preparations. Today she looks back and says: "Tell me one person who would not make this film under these conditions." There were, of course, many people who would not make such a film under any conditions and who fled Nazi Germany so that they would not be ordered to do so. But Riefenstahl stayed in Germany, demanded conditions that she felt would insure her artistic independence, and made the film; in so doing, she made the decision that, in public opinion, was to ruin her career.

In 1936, Leni Riefenstahl was commissioned by the International Olympics Committee (not by the Nazi Party) to make *Olympia* (1938), the official film record of the 1936 Olympic Games in Berlin. Both *Triumph of the Will* and *Olympia* are great works of the nonfiction film art, yet despite Riefenstahl's achievements, she never again had the opportunity to undertake projects as vast or as ambitious. After the Second World War began, the Nazi party had no use for her talents as a filmmaker.[2] In 1939, she produced short training films on sports, based on out-takes from *Olympia,* and once again she made plans to film the classic of German romanticism, Heinrich von Kleist's *Penthesilea,* but this passionate love story about an Amazon queen—with whom she says she identified "spiritually"—was never realized on film. Between 1939 and 1943, she developed other film projects, but none of them was ever realized.

From the beginning of her career, Riefenstahl wanted only to be an artist. It seems clear that her political sensibilities were naive, to say the least. Her persistent efforts to return to her own film projects, most notably *Tiefland* and *Penthesilea,* became something of an obsession with her; although most of *Tiefland* was filmed between 1940 and 1945, it was not completed and released until 1954. The end of the military conflict in 1945 marked the beginning of many years of personal hardship for Leni Riefenstahl. Though she was not a member of the Nazi party, she was arrested and imprisoned by the allied powers because of her films about the party and her associations with Hitler and other party officials. In 1948 and again in 1952 (the latter at her own request to further clear her name), she went through denazification proceedings. These were administrative and judicial hearings by specially appointed boards, not trials for people convicted of war crimes or of criminal acts. In both instances, she was identified as a "mere follower" of the Nazi party, and she proved to the satisfaction of the proceedings that her career during the Third Reich had been artistic rather than political. She was declared innocent of any political activity that would warrant punishment, and was absolved of any official penalties.

Despite acquittal and clearance, Leni Riefenstahl has paid the unofficial penalty of public shame for her former political associations. Evidently she does not agree that art can be used as a moral and ideological tool, nor does she appear to have any qualms about having created a celluloid shrine to Hitler and the Nazis. *Triumph of the Will* is surprisingly free of reference to the specific evils which we associate with the Nazi doctrine; the speeches, for example, have been edited to the most general statements about growth and progress. There is no reference anywhere in the film to extermination of the Jews or to conquest of the world. But according to twentieth century standards of humanism and democracy, the most insidious aspects of the film are its depiction of the individual as an unidentified part of a regimented mass and its adulatory and uncritical presentation of Hitler and the party, and, by our inference, all that they have come to stand for. Its most dangerous propagandistic insinuation is that emotion is superior to reason. Nonetheless, the film is a visual, sensual, kinetic, and cinematic marvel. In short, *Triumph of the Will,* like *Birth of a Nation,* embodies an overwhelming contradiction: it is cinematically dazzling and ideologically vicious. In 1965, Riefenstahl stated: "I have never done anything I didn't want to do, and nothing I've ever been ashamed of."³ Such a statement seems consistent with her notions of artistic independence and with her apparent naivete about the moral implications of her art.

With official clearance in 1952, Riefenstahl made a strong effort to reestablish herself as a filmmaker, but her many projects since then reflect a kind of escapism, a desire to run away from a real world which had condemned her and had withdrawn its support. In 1954, she completed *Tiefland,* a romantic tale of poor peasants who rebel against their oppressive landlords. Their struggle, with its Marxist implications, is symbolized on one side by a two-legged werewolf (the landlord) and one the other by four-legged predators (the wolves who attack the peasants' sheep). Set in eighteenth century Spain, it is a rich costume drama, notable for the strength of its story and for Riefenstahl's direction and performance as Martha, the gypsy dancer. In 1956, she discovered Africa, a discovery that was to change and, in her words, to revitalize her life. And while it may seem another attempt at escaping the postwar wreckage of her career, her interest in African tribal life follows her lifelong interest in the bold and the heroic. Her project titled *Schwarze Fracht* (*Black Cargo*), a semifictional documentary about slave traffic in modern Africa, was abandoned for various personal and financial reasons. Since 1962 she has been working to complete a color documentary film (to be titled *The Last of the Nuba*) about the life of tribes in the Sudan, and she has published a book of her still photographs on this spectacular tribe.

Leni Riefenstahl has become a legend and a *cause célèbre,* but her reputation should also be that of a great artist, one of the few truly great innovators in the art of the nonfiction film. Each of her four major films—*The Blue Light, Triumph of the Will, Olympia,* and *Tiefland*—reveals a different aspect of her style and of her cinematic mastery of the heroic form. Each is an expression of her fervently romantic imagination and of her beliefs in the abstract force of power, in physical beauty, in primitive ritual, and in the strength of ordinary people. Each film was made under extraordinary circumstances, and each was an adventure in itself. But despite her considerable achievement, Riefenstahl is generally regarded as the director who glorified Hitler, a Nazi if only by association. And despite her efforts and those of her supporters to create a climate in which the public might fairly evaluate her work, she remains a figure of scorn and shame, boycotted and banned. This is the paradox of Leni Riefenstahl and the ironic reward of a lifetime which she thought was devoted to artistic integrity and independence.

the production

The Making of *Triumph of the Will*

The 1934 Nazi party rally was called "Party Day of Unity" and "Party Day of Power," and it was planned to be an even larger, more impressive spectacle than the previous ones. The architectural and logistical planning for the anticipated 700,000 visitors to medieval Nuremberg ranged from a vast city of tents constructed to house and feed them, to the mammoth halls and stadia built for their meetings. However, the 1934 meeting was not staged solely for Riefenstahl's cameras. Since the rally was an annual event, it was staged for the cameras only to the extent that most political conventions in the United States are staged for the television cameras.[4] Party officials planned a series of spectacular events which would demonstrate party unity and power under Hitler's leadership; however, neither those events nor the film tell the truth about Germany or the Nazis. By late 1933, German society had been divided and shattered by political persecution and terrorism, including the establishment of detention camps for political prisoners. But since none of that was reflected outwardly in the events of Nuremberg, none of it appears in the film. Riefenstahl's film does not capture what, historically, we have come to see as the central experience of Nazism in 1934. But her task was to make a film of the party rally, not a documentary of prevailing social conditions or a statement of party philosophy. Her film is true to the reality of that rally, however dishonest and misleading that meeting may have been. But more than a mere record of events, it is a cinematic expression of the Nazi mystique.

Riefenstahl's claim that she had only two weeks to plan and organize the production of *Triumph of the Will* seems incredible, considering the size of the rally, the variety of its events, and the numbers in her crew. However, two weeks does seem to have been all the time she had; moreover, it seems to have been sufficient. Because of this short schedule and because, as she says, she had hoped to be relieved of the assignment, she did not give the planners of the rally any instructions for accommodating her production staff. Afterward, she complained that every possible obstacle was placed in her path; but according to the promotion booklet for the film, there was considerable cooperation between the authorities and the film crew. Aside from the predictable claims of press agents, *Hinter den Kulissen Des Reichsparteitagfilms* (*Behind the Scenes of the Reich's Party Rally Film*) is a reliable source of information about the size and composition of the crew and the method in which the film was shot.[5] As indicated in one of the main titles, *Triumph of the Will* was "produced by orders of the *Führer.*" It was financed and distributed by Ufa, the major German film company, which was sympathetic to the party but not under its direct control. The film was produced by Riefenstahl's company (Leni Riefenstahl Studio-Film) and it is registered in that name in the *Bundesarchiv* at Koblenz in Germany.

The scope of the production has prompted considerable speculation about the size of the crew and its resources, and so something of a legend has grown up around the film. But while the size of the crew is impressive, there is nothing really extraordinary about their use or placement of the cameras. When one considers the versatility and flexibility of the camera work in Dziga Vertov's *The Man With the Movie Camera* (1929), the achievements of Riefenstahl's large crew are unimpressive, although their intentions were different. Riefenstahl's statements vary regarding the number of cameramen involved and she has said that it was made "with very primitive means" and that it "was a very cheap film," costing only 280,000 marks, approximately $110,600 in 1934 (Delahaye, p. 391). The crew consisted of 172 people, including 16 cameramen and 16 camera assistants, under the direction of Sepp Allgeier. The camera crew used 30 cameras, and they were backed up by a team of 29 newsreel cameramen who were assigned to obtain supplementary footage. The cameramen were dressed as SA men, so that they would not stand out in the crowd; this appears to have been an effective foresight, for while there are at least 12 sequences in the film where cameras are momentarily noticeable, we are not aware of the crew working around them. In addition to the cameramen, there was a sound crew, a team of guards from the SA and SS, field police, and miscellaneous staff to handle the lighting and electrical arrangements. Transportation was a major consideration, and 22 chauffeur-driven cars were assigned to the production crew. The 172-person production staff breaks down as follows:

10 technical staff
36 cameramen & assistants
 9 aerial photographers
17 newsreel crew
12 newsreel crew from Tobis company
17 lighting crew
 2 still photographers
26 drivers
37 watchmen and security force
 4 labor service
 2 office.

The crew worked around the clock for seven days and nights, often accomplishing what appear to have been last-minute miracles in the placement of their equipment. Throughout this effort there was no means of central communication with the production headquarters and, in Riefenstahl's words, each cameraman was his own director, left to himself to organize and to choose what he would shoot. By way of instruction, she told each man only to avoid unimportant details but to leave nothing out. It is a measure of her knowledge of photography and her skill in selection and organization of personnel that she was able to trust the intuitive judgment of her cameramen. She estimates, however, that 50 percent of the completed film is composed of footage from Allgeier's own camera.

The one idea that guided Riefenstahl was that the film be composed of "moving images," not the "static" images of the newsreels she deplored. Rather humbly, she admits that "maybe this was an interesting approach"; it was more than interesting, however, for it is a brilliant solution to the problem of providing kinetic, cinematic energy to essentially static events. Riefenstahl claims that Nazi officials refused to implement many of her plans for placement of cameras and that she was able to obtain an elevator and tracks for the cameras only through the intervention of Rudolph Hess, to whom she appealed. While she claims that Goebbels was behind the obstruction, there is little actual evidence in the film itself that her crew was prevented from obtaining favorable positions for closeups or any other kind of shots. Indeed, it is the directness and immediacy of the photography that leads some to believe that the action of the film was staged for the cameras.

The cameramen recorded almost sixty-one hours of film from almost every imaginable angle: from rooftops, windows, gutters, and eye-level; and from a variety of moving devices, including roller skates, airplanes, dirigibles, fire-truck ladders, automobiles, conventional camera dollies, and an elevator. The visual quality of the film varies, in part, because of these overall conditions and the use of different speeds of black and white film stock. Despite the remarkable intimacy achieved in many of the shots, few of the people in the film acknowledge the presence of the cameras, which record everything from the playful leisure games of soldiers to Hitler's unnerving stare as he greets members of his troops.

Riefenstahl edited the film herself, giving the task her total attention for almost five months. She compares the process of editing with dancing and says that she learned much about artistic shape, movement, and rhythm from her early training. A true *auteur,* she says that the completed film was a realization of her own vision. All the sound, with the exception of the speeches, was synchronized in the studio in the incredibly short period of three days. The lack of extensive magnetic recording equipment, plus the physical difficulties of the production, made it impossible to do much direct sound recording. All the speeches were recorded directly as they were delivered, except Streicher's; she says an equipment failure made it necessary to rerecord the one sentence from his speech used in the film. The sound track is a rich mixture of actual speeches, music, cheers, and some effects created in the studio. But the aural power of the film does not lie in the speeches, but rather in the music.

The musical score was composed by Herbert Windt, and Riefenstahl praises him as a "genius . . . the great luck for this film and for *Olympia* and *Tiefland."* They worked together closely on the synchronization, creating some of the crowd sounds themselves, with help of friends and assistants. Because the cameras used in the filming were not motor-driven, there were always problems synchronizing music to the variable speeds of the footage contributed by the many cameramen. To overcome this problem in the long parade scene (scene 11), Riefenstahl herself conducted the studio orchestra to match the tempo of the music to the cadence of the marching troops. Windt combines a few Wagnerian themes with many neo-Wagnerian heroic themes, German folk melodies, martial music, and party anthems to create a score of continual variety and interest. He evokes emotion with the moving strains of "I Had a Comrade" and solidarity with the "Horst Wessel" song, the official anthem of the Nazi party. Riefenstahl says that the "secret" of *Olympia* is sound; the "secrets" of the power and originality of *Triumph of the Will* are Windt's score and Riefenstahl's consummate skill in editing and juxtaposition of sight and sound.

Triumph of the Will was presented in its premiere performance on March 28, 1935, at the *Ufa-Palast-am-Zoo,* Berlin's largest theatre. Hitler was in the audience and liked the film; it was the first time he had seen it. While Ufa had a good success with the film in the larger cities of Germany, it was not successful with the general public and was not used very widely as propaganda. Nazi officials objected that it was too artistic, and some complained that they were not well-represented. Regardless of his feelings about Riefenstahl, Goebbels praised the fiilm and awarded it the National Film Prize during the "Festival of the Nation" on May 1, 1935. In addition to the German prize, the film was awarded the *Diplome de Grand Prix,* or Grand Prize, on July 4, 1937, at the *Exposition Internationale des Arts et des Techniques* in Paris, although Riefenstahl's appearance in France to receive the award was protested by French workers. Since the second world war, German law has forbidden the screening of any films of Hitler or the Nazi party. For this reason, the film is not screened publicly in Germany, but it is widely shown in other European countries, in Great Britain, and in the United States.

analysis

In *Triumph of the Will,* Leni Riefenstahl imposes her vision upon realistic footage to achieve a wholly unique form of nonfiction film: the propaganda documentary. The film is more an achievement of editing than photography, and while editing implies selection, organization, and arrangement, it also implies deletion, emphasis, and distortion. Riefenstahl edited the footage to achieve two basic goals: the glorification of the Nazi party and the deification of Adolf Hitler. Some viewers may question the sincerity of the mass emotion expressed at the rallies, or find themselves alienated by the party rhetoric, but most agree on the cinematic power of the film. Ultimately, the modern audience is stunned both by the film's artistic power and by its political content.

As Wagner, Bruckner, and Mahler before her, Leni Riefenstahl gives artistic expression to an heroic conception of life. She develops the heroic elements with restraint, but emphasizes the idea that Hitler will restore Germany to heights of ancient heroic grandeur. This is directly evident in a number of scenes, but most apparent in the strong opening scene; it is reflected in Speer's severe architectural setting for the rally; in the many shots of Hitler photographed against the sun or sky; in the mists, clouds, and smoke; in the trappings and heraldry; in the processions, festivals, and rallies; and in the awe and wonder and enthusiasm of the crowds. The world of the Nazi leaders seems like Valhalla, a place apart, surrounded by clouds and mist, peopled by heroes, and ruled from above by gods. Much of the effectiveness of Riefenstahl's reinterpretation of German myth relies on the interplay of the heroic visual image and the heroic musical score. Hitler was passionately devoted to Richard Wagner's great *Ring der Nibelungen,* but Herbert Windt does not emphasize the obvious by using themes directly from Wagner's operas in his score (except in the rare instances as noted in the following analysis); instead, he relies on the audience's familiarity with Wagner and creates a new heroic score which evokes the Wagnerian world without imitating it. Contrary to what one might expect, the musical references are not to the operas in the *Ring* cycle but rather to Wagner's *Die Meistersinger von Nürnberg.* By mixing Wagner, folk music, and songs of the Nazi party, Windt suggests the continuation of an ancient musical tradition.

While the principal concern of the film is the portrayal of Hitler, the secondary concerns are to demonstrate party unity and solidarity and to display civilian and military strength. The film presents a record of many groups, from colorful peasants representing the oldest German traditions in dress and music, to the youngest boys representing the hope of the future. Included also are the elite secret troops, the labor service, the leaders of various party factions, and the women in the crowds. There were women in various Nazi services, but they are rarely seen in the film. Perhaps never before—with the possible exception of Eisenstein's *Potemkin* (1925)—and never since in a film have the spirit and consciousness of a political movement been paraded before the cameras in such a revealing way. The slow, stately rhythm of the film is that of the imperial or religious procession. From beginning to end, we are aware of movement, a metaphor for progress. With great care and often great subtlety, the film coverage moves from event to event, capturing the vitality and variety of six days in two hours of superb footage.

The narrative continuity of *Triumph of the Will* does not match the chronological sequence of the actual events of the sixth Nazi party rally, nor does the film include everything. To achieve the internal dramatic rhythm and progression of the film, Riefenstahl rearranged the order of events. For example, the meeting of the Women's Association is not in the film, and the series of speech excerpts in scene 4 derives from several meetings, not from one as is suggested by the film. With the exception of the music, she has not added anything that did not actually occur; through her photography and editing, she has transformed the prosaic happenings into cinematic poetry.

According to the film, the 1934 party rally was not the platform for deciding policy, or the occasion for lunches, dinners, receptions, or dances; and even Riefenstahl complained about the lack of variety in the activity. Nonetheless, the events are spectacular and Riefenstahl makes the spectacle exciting. She keeps the cameras moving as much as possible, especially when the subject is not in motion. Even Hitler's speeches are transformed by the moving camera and the montage. Through visual movement and variety, we are involved in the speeches; moreover, we are compelled by the close-ups to look at the speaker and not necessarily to listen to his banal oratory.

There is movement everywhere in *Triumph of the Will,* for even such inanimate objects as buildings and flags are given life. We see Nuremberg through a window; as the camera moves closer for a better view, some unseen force opens the window (a few moments later, a hand opens another window); the camera pans across the rooftops, recording fluttering banners and smoking chimneys. Through aerial photography, Riefenstahl relieves the heaviness of marching columns by picturing them as a gently wavering line moving far below. When Hitler passes crowds in his open car, we go along, for a camera is mounted on a car moving alongside his, and we are involved in passing his car and in watching it catch up to ours.

The film is divided into parts or movements, each linked to the others by narrative and by theme and motif; and each section of the film has a different style. Yet the overall film is a triumph of organic unity. Themes are stated and restated, motifs are introduced and repeated, but all the individual elements of the film are subordinate to an overall structure which expresses and embodies the director's particular vision. All of the parts come together to create a whole, a crescendo of themes at the end, as the film moves from dawn to dawn, from air to earth, and back to air at the end.

This analysis is based on the print of *Triumph of the Will* circulated by the Museum of Modern Art, a print which corresponds almost exactly to prints held by the Imperial War Museum in London, England, the *Bundesarchiv* at Koblenz, Germany, and to the print in Riefenstahl's archive. Of course, there are no English subtitles on the original film, and none appear on any of the prints circulated by the Museum of Modern Art; however, Contemporary Films/McGraw-Hill, the only American distributor authorized by Riefenstahl to rent the film, circulates prints with English subtitles, but these subtitles are incomplete and therefore inaccurate. The translation of the German speeches which appears here was prepared by Dr. Renata von Stoephasius of Richmond College of the City University of New York. In keeping with the objective of this study, a special effort has been made to provide as faithful and as literal a translation of the speeches as possible. For purposes of this analysis, I have discussed the film as if it were divided into twelve scenes; in the film, the scenes are separated only by such cinematic transitions as fade-outs and dissolves.

SCENE 1

Triumph of the Will opens dramatically. The screen is dark for 1:05 minutes while the musical overture establishes a romanticized heroic mood; the first images are of the eagle and the swastika, symbols of the Nazi party, followed by the titles. These titles create a cumulative effect by focusing the immediate moment against an historical background, and they provide the necessary literal background for the opening of the film narrative.

Underscored with an orchestral version of the "Horst Wessel" song mixed with sounds of the airplane engine, the narrative literally and visually begins in the clouds in Hitler's plane on its way to Nuremberg. Through the pilot's window, we see clouds; the sun strikes the edges of dark clouds, and the nose of the plane appears. The plane is fully visible against the clouds; the sunlight becomes brighter and lightens the masses of clouds. We do not see Hitler, the pilot, or any of the accompanying party. Shots of the plane in the air over the city are intercut with aerial shots of the columns of the "faithful" marching into the city; the most impressive of these shots records the shadow of the plane as it passes over the men, as if blessing them. (This image is recalled in Federico Fellini's *La Dolce Vita* [1959] with the helicopter towing the statue of Christ across Rome.) The immediate effect of the prologue is breathtaking, for in a matter of minutes Riefenstahl has conveyed the solitary power, the isolated strength, and the mystery of the Nazi party and its *Führer*. Party symbolism associated Hitler with an eagle and the film often juxtaposes shots of the eagle with shots of the *Führer*, but here the approach of the plane—like an eagle which casts its shadow on its grounded prey—adds an ominous, and perhaps unintended, meaning to the *Führer's* arrival.

The symbols of the party were the symbols of the state, and

Nazi propaganda experts used sign, symbol, and song to focus and to define party strength and significance. In *Triumph of the Will,* the repeated use of the eagle, the swastika, and the "Horst Wessel" song both induces and helps to explain the emotional involvement of the leaders and their followers. Through Nazi politics and propaganda, German romanticism and mysticism were revitalized and became a new emotional experience. This experience relies on several factors: the collective emotional frenzy of the crowd; the elite, secret cadre of their leaders; and the use of verbal and non-verbal techniques, including symbol, sound, pageantry, lighting, and color. Hitler was the most recognizable and potent element in Nazi propaganda. Despite his shortness, he was a forbidding figure; although his speeches never support his awesome public image, he knew how repetition and emphasis could incite and excite a crowd. This inconsistency between Hitler's undeniable power as a visual and human symbol of the party and his unimpressive appearance and speaking ability betrays an overall weakness in Riefenstahl's vision: the discernible gap between historical reality and cinematic illusion.

After the opening sequence has associated Hitler with the eagle, the clouds, and the gods, a brief montage shows him for the first time as he steps from his airplane. Now the marching troops, the cheering crowds, and the excitement and anticipation are all explained as he becomes the symbolic and visual focus of the rally and of the film. Hitler's car and accompanying motorcade move rapidly through the city streets lined with cheering crowds. The counterpoint composition of this sequence places Hitler in the foreground of the frame, in focus, while the crowd is in the background, slightly out of focus. His half-figure is photographed against the sun, so that a halo effect is achieved in profile. Close-up shots of Hitler are intercut with shots of the crowd, taken from a moving car. One remarkable close-up reinforces the messianic presence of the *Führer* by capturing the sun as it is refracted in the upraised palm of his hand. At one point, in what must have been planned for the film, Hitler's car stops so that he can accept a gift of flowers offered by a little girl who is held up by her mother. Mother and daughter salute the leader, other smiling children begin to cheer, and the procession resumes. The cumulative effect of this montage results in yet another aspect of Riefenstahl's portrait of Hitler: his personal presence. People lean from the windows of flag-decorated buildings, and even a cat on a windowsill seems to stop licking itself just so it too can watch the motorcade. In this sequence—indeed, through the film itself—there is a fine feeling for the city of Nuremberg.

When Hitler reaches his hotel, the visual emphasis shifts from him to his troops, to close-up shots of their faces, insignia, belts, and hands linked together as a protective force against the surging crowds; a ground-level shot of the men's knee boots completes the montage. These shots of the stance and insignia of Hitler's troops create a threatening atmosphere and develop another source of the *Führer's* power, not in the cheering crowds of ordinary citizens, but in the regimented ranks of his soldiers. And the shots of the boots only help to reinforce a motif that is developed completely later in the film: the legions of men who march behind the *Führer*. The scene fades out with the crowd's enthusiastic shouts of *"Heil!"*

In this first scene of *Triumph of the Will,* Leni Riefenstahl uses Hitler's triumphant entry into Nuremberg to establish that he is a man above men, as well as a man among men, and that he is a leader whose power is vested both in his personal popularity and in the combined strength of his faithful troops.

SCENE 2

The second scene, a torchlit band concert in front of Hitler's hotel, is a transition between the demonstrative power of the first scene and the excitement of the third; it is thus less interesting cinematically and thematically. It begins with shots of banners and flags fluttering from standards on nearby buildings. Flags are one of Riefenstahl's most persistent and effective motifs and they suggest a lightness and transcience which is in direct and, perhaps, ironic counterpoint to the equally persistent images of a more fixed and stable nature: eagles and the swastika. In the dim light, we see the conductor, the band, and the troops that gently restrain the surging crowds as they listen to a program of military march music. Predominant in the flickering light and shadow of the torches are various flags, insignia, and a lighted swastika and sign—*Heil Hitler*—on the front of the hotel. Storm troopers are silhouetted against the light, and Hitler and his party listen to the music as they stand on the hotel balcony and survey the scene.

The overall impression is one of calm and reflection. To this point, Hitler has been viewed as a figure of power, seen briefly at the airfield, in a brisk motorcade, in the window of his hotel, and on the balcony in the dim light listening to the music. Accordingly, the tone of the film has been one of restrained enthusiasm. Now, this reflective nighttime scene foreshadows the excitement of the hundreds of thousands of visitors to Nuremberg for the spectacle to follow. The camera moves about the crowd recording a sense of anticipation, but the scene also contributes to the energy of theatrical suspense which helps to move the film forward.

SCENE 3

The first part of the third scene is the most graceful and serene moment in the film, and sets a mood of peace and tranquility. In the first moments of early morning no people are evident. The towers of the old town emerge dimly on the screen in the half light of dawn. The music is the hymn, "Awake! The dawn of day draws near" from act 3 of *Die Meistersinger von Nürnberg.* The camera pans across rooftops; a curtain is drawn back; a window opens; flags and banners flutter gently in the breeze; chimneys begin to smoke—all indicating that daily activity is beginning. The Pegnitz River reflects the buildings and arched bridges, and a camera mounted on a slowly moving boat records further views of the buildings, spires, and the bell tower. The morning light grows brighter as the chimes which conclude Wagner's music ring seven times to establish the hour.

The next long and carefully detailed sequence begins with a dissolve from the bell tower to an aerial view of the vast tent city built to house the troops and workers visiting Nuremberg for the rally. With this transition, the sound changing from hymns to morning trumpet calls, Riefenstahl links the preceding sequence of almost spiritual calm to a sequence of physical activity. At first, all is still; then, we see the thousands of men leave their tents and move around the grounds in the early morning light. The activity is underscored by the trumpets and drums of reveille, and by brisk, spirited military music. Here, as in *Olympia,* Riefenstahl is fascinated by vital, attractive men. Naked to the waist, the men here are busy washing, shaving, shining shoes, and helping to comb each other's hair. There is an evident friendly, cooperative spirit, and Riefenstahl's cameras capture a great deal of lively horseplay. The symbolic implications of the first two sequences of the third scene derive from Riefenstahl's handling of the dark and light imagery. In the preceding scene, at the band concert, all was calm and quiet; now, in this scene, in the brightness of the rising sun, the men are full of energy and vitality.

Their playful energy is next channeled into work, as the men sing work songs, light fires, and prepare breakfast; the songs are jovial and are accented by cheers and shouts as the men and boys line up for morning rations. While there are no visual references to Hitler in either of these sequences, perhaps the viewer is meant unconsciously to associate the morning sun with the sunlight that was refracted in his cupped palm during the motorcade sequence in the first scene. Yet once again there is a discernible gap between the reality Riefenstahl records and the illusion she hopes to project. The myth here suggests that the *Führer* descends from the clouds, a region of light, and brings light with him; in turn, this light becomes energy in the food that he provides to fuel the activity of his men. But in actuality the Nazi party behaves toward the men as if they were a herd of animals: the soldiers sleep on piles of straw, they wash in troughs, and they are fed out of buckets.

After the meal, the focus shifts from the men to boys in a rapid montage of youthful fun and games. This brilliantly edited sequence maintains a consistently high note of joviality, driven along by an excellent mix of songs, shouts, and cheers; although it was assembled in the studio, it effectively suggests that there is joy, fun, and friendship to be found in all aspects of communal activity, and in the life of the people under Hitler's rule. The sequence ends with a wipe-down, again a thematic and visual transition. In this instance, the visual transition also links groups of people—soldiers and peasants. Riefenstahl's intention, of course, is to demonstrate solidarity behind Hitler and the party.

The scene's third sequence begins with a man playing a concertina, leading a group of his countrymen; the shot recalls similar shots in Eisenstein's *Strike* (1924) and Dovzhenko's *Arsenal* (1929). The group of men, women, and children are on their way to Nuremberg for the day's activities; they are dressed in traditional costumes of various German districts, and many of them carry agricultural produce and implements. Here, again, is another example of the propaganda possibilities inherent in factual footage, and Riefenstahl reinforces the idea that she established earlier: that all people support Hitler—men, women, boys, and now the peasants bringing support from the outlying regions and farms. These happy, smiling people mingle with their musicians as they approach the city with their flower garlands and other harvest offerings. In addition to the idea of nationwide unity, there is a marked note of anticipation; here, in one of the subtlest transitions in the film, Hitler appears among the peasants, thereby suggesting that he was never far away from them. He leaves his hotel and immediately begins to greet them with handshakes and salutes, greeting and talking with individual people. When a young woman offers him some flowers, he refuses the gift, but his gesture is friendly. More important, the moment underscores the theme of this scene: Hitler is one of the people, but quite obviously he is apart from them too. He is the leader, and they are the workers; he is the focus of their efforts, and they bring gifts to him as a symbol of their work in his name, in the name of the state. The photography here captures the charm, informality, and gentleness of the moment, and is particularly effective in its intimate recording of the people's faces. But while certain persons appear as individuals, the group is still the group, representing the mass of people under Hitler's power. However informal he may appear, he is still the *Führer,* and the strength of that position is clearly demonstrated in the next sequence.

The fluidity of cinematic time bridges the gap between these third and fourth sequences, between the image of Hitler as folk hero and Hitler as troop leader, between the lilt of folk melodies and the melancholy themes of the "Horst Wessel" song. Here, Hitler reviews a group of young, stern flagbearers, and reinforces the seriousness of the moment by shaking hands with each of them. This sequence presents another very personal view of Hitler, but the parallels between this sequence and the previous one are clear; as with the farmers, he is in close, personal contact with a group of his followers, but he is also clearly their leader. After the review, Hitler salutes and enters a large open touring car; triumphal music underlines the grandeur of the moment as the car pulls away from the curb to begin a motorcade of party officials. We are brought directly into participation through a boy whose face is full of wonder and awe at the sight of Hitler's magnificent automobile. And yet we, like the boy, are part of the mass, in the crowd looking at the leader. With a single boy's salute, the scene fades out.

The shift here from the specific entity of the troops to the larger symbolic whole of the party leadership is significant because it serves to reinforce the strong connection between abstract symbol of the party itself and the specific men who form its ranks and lead its movement. The rapid exit in the big car is exciting in itself, but it also prepares a ceremonial mood for the following scene. Until now, Hitler has been pictured mostly in contrast to the crowds. Against various backgrounds, we have seen him—stern, friendly, in the distance, and in close-up—and we have seen the people— always as members of a mass united in its friendly welcome to the city. It is at this point that Riefenstahl begins to flex the political muscle of the film, to show the official magnitude of Hitler's power, to transform personal magnetism into political leadership.

SCENE 4

This scene records the opening congress of delegates, but the static set of speeches which compose it abruptly halts the rhythm and progression that have been established for the film. Here Riefenstahl's dynamic montage gives way to static propaganda necessities as the mythic world of her film yields to the prosaic meeting in the vast congress hall. The speeches are vague, over-blown, obligatory; like many political speeches, they reassure, confirm, and satisfy the listener rather than provoke him. In the excerpts from speeches by party officials, we see each man and hear the essence of his belief, deliberately general in content, delib-erately impassioned in delivery. There are no disturbing ideas, no reactionary proposals, and certainly no indication of the evil that was to come as a result of party policies.

The first speaker is Rudolf Hess, the Deputy Leader of the Nazi Party, dressed in the uniform of a storm trooper. In a mon-tage similar in sight and sound to those in the remainder of the scene, shots of Hess are intercut with shots of the listening crowd, of individuals, of insignia, of eagles and swastikas on poles and banners, and of a large sign at the opposite end of the hall which reads: *"Alles für Deutschland"* (Everything for Germany).

HESS: I am opening this, our sixth Party Congress, in respect-ful remembrance of Field Marshal, and President of the Reich, von Hindenburg, who has passed on into eternity. We remember the Field Marshal as the first soldier of the great war, and, thus, also remember our dead comrades.

I welcome the esteemed representatives of foreign countries who honor the party by their presence, and the party, in sincere friendship, welcomes especially the representatives of the mili-tary forces, now under the leadership of our *Führer.* My *Führer!* Around you are gathered the flags and banners of this National Socialism. Only when their cloth has worn thin will people, looking back, be able to understand fully the greatness of this time and conceive what you, my *Führer,* mean to Germany.

You are Germany. When you act, the nation acts; when you judge, the people judge. Our gratitude to you will be our pledge to stand by you for better and for worse, come what may! Thanks to your leadership, Germany will attain her aim to be the homeland of all the Germans of the world. You have guar-anteed our victory, and you are now guaranteeing our peace. *Heil Hitler! Sieg Heil! Sieg Heil! Sieg Heil!*

Hess' introductory speech literally sets the stage for a series of brief remarks by party officials. The first speaker is introduced by a fade in to a blurred title which then slowly "fires" into focus: "An excerpt from the *Führer's* proclamation, read to the audience by Wagner." (Adolf Wagner was the *Gauleiter,* or district leader, of Bavaria.) Title "fires" out of focus, dissolving into a medium shot of Wagner, who stands at the podium and reads the statement.

> WAGNER: No revolution could last forever without leading to total anarchy. Just as the world cannot exist on wars, nations cannot exist on revolutions. There is nothing great on this earth that has ruled the world for milleniums and was created in decades. The highest tree has had the longest period of growth. What has withstood centuries will also need centuries to become strong.

Following this, ten party leaders are heard; each is introduced by a title which "fires" into focus on his last name, and then "fires" out and dissolves into a medium or close-up shot of the speaker. The speakers are:

> Alfred Rosenberg, Reich Leader of Foreign Policy Office and Commissioner for Supervision of Ideological Education of the NSDAP
> Otto Dietrich, Reich Press Chief
> Fritz Todt, General Inspector for the German Road System
> Fritz Reinhardt, Head of Official NSDAP School for Orators
> Walter Darré, Reich Minister of Agriculture
> Julius Streicher, Publisher of *Der Stürmer* (The Stormtrooper) and *Gauleiter* of Franken
> Robert Ley, Leader of the Reich Labor Front
> Hans Frank, Reich Minister of Justice
> Paul Joseph Goebbels, Reich Minister of Propaganda
> Konstantin Hierl, Leader of the Reich Labor Service

This lengthy scene significantly distorts reality in at least three ways. First, it is a compilation of speeches from various meetings, not just from this opening session. Second, it presents only bland excerpts, which are an unfaithful representation of the actual oratory. Third, it unites the speeches with motifs of hope, progress, and unity, bending the actual substance of each speaker's remarks to the general purpose of the film's propaganda.

ROSENBERG: It is our unshakable belief in ourselves, it is our hope for today's special youth, who, tempestuously charging forward, will one day be called upon to continue the efforts begun in the stormy years of the 1918 Munich Revolution, an event which gripped all of Germany and the historical importance of which is already being embodied today by the entire German nation.

DIETRICH: Truth is the foundation on which the power of the press stands and falls, and our only demand of the press, also the foreign press, is that they report the truth about Germany.

TODT: The construction of the autobahn system has begun in fifty-one places in the nation. Although this is just the beginning, 52,000 men are already working on the construction of these roads, and another 100,000 men are employed at construction sites, in supplying the building trade with its materials, and in bridge construction.

REINHARDT: Wherever one looks, construction is in progress, improvements are being made, and new values created. And wherever one looks, since last year, there is industrious activity, activity which will continue in the future.

DARRE: The continued welfare of our farmers is the first condition for the success of our industry, our domestic trade, and the German export trade.

STREICHER: A nation that does not value its racial purity will perish.

LEY: One thought alone must dominate all our work: to make the German worker an upstanding, proud citizen enjoying equal rights with the rest of the nation.

FRANK: As head of the German judiciary, I can only say that since the National Socialist legal system is the foundation of the National Socialist state, for us our supreme *Führer* is also our supreme judge. And since we know how sacred the principles of justice are to our *Führer*, we can assure you, fellow citizens, that your life and existence is safe in this National Socialist state of order, freedom, and law.

GOEBBELS: May the bright flame of our enthusiasm never go out. This flame alone gives light and warmth to the creative art of modern political propaganda. This art rises from the depths of the nation and, in order to search for its roots and find its power, it must again return to these depths. It may be all right to have power that is based on guns; however, it is better and more gratifying to win the heart of a nation and to keep it.

HIERL: The German people today are mentally and spiritually ready for the introduction of general labor service conscription. We await the order of the *Führer*.

While Hierl's brief statement marks the formal end of the fourth scene, a dissolve to a close-up of the Labor Front flag maintains the transition between this scene—held at night in the congress hall—and the next scene—held by day at an outdoor rally. Again, Riefenstahl has altered time and space to create the visual and thematic sense of unity and solidarity in party ranks.

SCENE 5

The scene is a vast outdoor rally of members of the Labor Service on the *Zeppelinwiese;* it opens with a continued close-up of the Labor Service flag which ended the previous scene. Hitler steps to a raised platform; Hitler and Hierl address each other; Hierl addresses the massed troops of workers.

HIERL: My *Führer!* 52,000 laborers await your order.
HITLER: *Heil,* workers!
WORKERS: *Heil,* my *Führer!*
LEADER: Present shovels! At ease!

As if they were soldiers, the massed forces stand at attention with their shovels, instead of guns, and then, at ease; the overall effect of the scene is militaristic. Just as the workers were apparently rehearsed in their performance here, so Riefenstahl's cameramen must also have been rehearsed because, in contrast to shots of other mass rallies, the photography here seems designed to capture the maximum effect. The cameras glide smoothly on tracks, and careful close-ups of various speakers lack the informal quality of close-up shots elsewhere in the film. This entire sequence seems to have been staged, photographed, and recorded for the benefit of the cameras.

A ceremony of loyalty begins. Shots of Hitler and Hierl watching the demonstration are intercut with shots of the workers; a leader addresses the workers and they answer in unison.

> WORKERS: Here we stand; we are ready to carry Germany into a new era. Germany!
> LEADER: Comrade, where are you from?
> WORKER: From Friesland.
> LEADER: And you, comrade?
> WORKER: From Bavaria.
> LEADER: And you?
> WORKER: From the Kaiserstuhl.
> LEADER: And you?
> WORKERS: From Pomerania, and from Königsberg, from Silesia, from the seaside, from the Black Forest, from Dresden, from the Danube, from the Rhine, and from the Saar.

In the following passage, the leader and workers alternate words and phrases:

> One nation, one leader, one Reich—Germany! Today, we are all working together in the bogs, quarries, in the sandpits, on the dikes of the North Sea. We plant trees, rustling forests. We build roads from village to village, from town to town. We create new acreage for the farmer. Fields and forests, acres and bread—for Germany!

In a solemn ceremony, various flags are dipped to the ground in honor of those who fell in the first world war; as before, there is an avid enthusiasm in the leader's eyes:

> We did not stand in the trenches, nor did we stand under the drumfire of the grenades, and, nevertheless, we are soldiers, with our hammers, axes, shovels, hoes, and spades—we are the young troops of this Reich!

A band plays the sad melody, "I Had a Comrade," and each time a battlefield is mentioned, another flag is dipped.

> WORKERS: As formerly at Langemark, at Tannenberg, at Liège, at Verdun, at the Somme, the Düna, in Flanders, in the west, in the east, in the south, on land, on the seas, and in the skies— "Comrades, by Red Front and reaction, killed . . ."[6] You are not dead, you are alive—in Germany!

The idea that life comes out of death supports the larger idea of a German renaissance under Hitler—an idea stated in the opening titles—but it also hints at the darker idea that war is necessary for the continuation of Germany's life. In addition, the workers are made to feel that life and death at home are as important as life and death on foreign battlefields. The workers demonstrate this idea with their songs, choral speeches, and marches, and Hitler reinforces it with the following speech. While Hitler is speaking, we see him from various angles, from a distance, and in close-up; these shots are combined into an overall montage including close-ups and moving shots of the listening workers, and close-ups of belts, insignia, and flags. Hitler speaks with emotion and emphasizes important points with a raised fist.

> HITLER: Men of the Labor Service! For the first time, you appear here in this form for inspection before me and therefore before the whole German nation. You represent a great idea, and we know that for millions of our fellow citizens the concept of labor will no longer be a dividing one but a uniting one, and

that no longer will there be anybody in Germany who will regard manual labor less highly than any other form of labor. The whole nation will have to go through the training you have gone through. A time will come when no German will be able to join the community of this nation unless he has been a member of your community first. And you know that not only the hundreds of thousands at Nuremberg are looking at you, but, at this moment, that all of Germany is seeing you for the first time. And I know just as you are serving Germany in loyal devotion, Germany today sees, in proud joy, its sons marching in your ranks.

The discipline and order of this scene reaches a climax with columns of marching workers who sing "We are work-soldiers" as they move toward the camera. As a group, they have gone through their maneuvers and have spoken their lines in unison; still a regimented group, they move with determination, and their movement suggests that they have been inspired, by the *Führer's* words, to go off to work.

SCENE 6

As lively and as loud as the previous scene was solemn, this nighttime rally of storm troopers is punctuated by the sound of drums and the music of *"Volk ans Gewehr."* The moving camera records flags, banners, torches, and storm troopers who are often seen in silhouette in the smoky light; in contrast, the main speaker appears in spotlight. The shadowy excitement of this scene provides considerable dramatic material which Riefenstahl heightens with a juxtaposition of light and dark images and with the use of the moving camera. The SA leader Viktor Lutze speaks to the assembled storm troopers.

> LUTZE: Comrades! Many of you who are here tonight know me from those first years of our movement when I marched with you in your rank and file as an SA man. I am as much of an SA man now as I was then. We SA men have known only one thing: fidelity to, and fighting for the *Führer.*

This brief speech relates this equally brief scene to the film as a whole; Lutze reminds the assembled storm troopers that he is still one of them—a pointed reminder that he was not killed in the massacre of SA leader Ernst Röhm and his followers. But his position on the platform raises him above the men, and repeats, on a smaller scale of authority, the relationship of the leader to the group, of the one to the many. Thus, Riefenstahl returns to a major theme of her film: the role of the solitary leader in authority in contrast to the roles of the obedient men beneath him.

This rally seems to have been planned more for pleasure than for political purposes. In the absence of speeches, there is a large display of aerial fireworks, bonfires, blazing pinwheels, as well as the random movement of men carrying flaming torches. In a daringly successful attempt to focus our attention on the pyrotechnic display, Riefenstahl has optically reversed the opening images so that the first burst implodes, rather than explodes, thus drawing the eye toward the center of the frame; this initial brief implosion is followed by an explosion, and the display continues. The effect recalls a similar moment in Ruttmann's *Berlin: The Symphony of a Great City* (1927). Lutze and his men watch the display; other storm troopers are shown singing, chanting, laughing, and throwing wood onto the fires. The scene fades out as the final fireworks die.

The scene's overall mood is gay and restless; however, a note of vulgarity and earthiness here hints at something darker. The dim setting, the blazing bonfires, and the smoking torches make a perfect theatrical setting for the storm troopers. While the scene is relatively brief, it functions in two ways: to preserve a record of the rally and, perhaps more important, to establish a contrast to the next scene. Here, the dark, smoky mystique of the SA rally reinforces the men's blood brotherhood and suggests their mythic origins in fire; in the next scene, a sunlit youth rally, the emphasis is on the same political idea—massed troops in support of the *Führer*—but the atmosphere is different. The boys are fresh and uninitiated; they know nothing of smoke, fire, or purges of disloyal members from their ranks. Here, as in many places in the film, Riefenstahl juxtaposes light with dark, leaders with troops, boys with men, peace with war, and the kinetic with the static.

SCENE 7

This scene records a huge daytime rally of the Hitler Youth groups in the vast Youth Stadium; it provides, in almost every way, a direct and dramatic contrast to the preceding scene. The previous scene took place in semi-darkness, but this is staged in bright sunlight; before, the participants were the rugged men of Hitler's SA; now, they are the fresh-faced, well-scrubbed and suitably blond and Aryan boys of the youth forces; earlier, the revelry was high, but now the proceedings are disciplined, formal, and serious.

Hitler's entry into the stadium is recorded in a montage which reveals the rhythm and detail that Riefenstahl extends to even the most basic subject. The montage captures the excitement and anticipation in the crowd and fairly bristles with activity as Hitler receives the ovations and welcome of the crowd. Baldur von Schirach, leader of the Hitler Youth, introduces Hitler.

VON SCHIRACH: My *Führer*. My comrades. Again we experience the hour that makes us happy and proud. At your order, my *Führer*, a young people is facing you—a young generation that does not know class and caste. Because you are the example of greatest unselfishness in this nation, this young generation wants to be unselfish too. Because you embody the concept of fidelity for us, we want to be faithful too. Adolf Hitler, the leader of German youth, will speak.

HITLER: My German youth! After one year, I have an opportunity to welcome you here again. Those of you who stand here in this stadium are only a small segment of the masses who stand outside, all over Germany. We wish that you, German boys and girls [there are virtually no girls evident in the film], absorb all that we expect of Germany in times to come. We want to be a united nation, and you, my youth, are to become this nation. In the future, we do not wish to see classes and cliques, and you must not allow them to develop among you. One day, we want to see *one* nation, and you must educate yourselves for it; we wish this people to be obedient, and you have to practice obedience; we wish this people to be peace-loving, but also brave, and you will have to be peace-loving. You must therefore be peace-loving and courageous at the same time. We do not want this nation to become soft; instead, it should be hard, and you will have to harden yourselves while you are young. You must learn to accept deprivations without ever collapsing. Regardless of whatever we create and do, we shall pass away, but in you, Germany will live on; and when nothing is left of us, you will have to hold up the banner which some time ago we lifted out of nothingness. And I know it cannot be otherwise because you are flesh of our flesh, blood of our blood, and your young minds are filled with the same spirit that dominates us. You cannot be but united with us. And when the great columns of our movement march victoriously through Germany today, I know that you will join these columns. And we know that Germany is before us, within us, and behind us.

Hitler delivers this speech with deep emotion and dramatic gestures, emphasizing the theme of the rally: that the participants "who stand in the stadium are only a small segment of the masses who stand outside, all over Germany." This idea is reinforced by the montage in which Hitler is pictured alone, in juxtaposition to the boys, who are seen individually, in groups of two or three, and in long shots of the whole group. They boys seem as stern as their leader, but they break their attentive listening with frequent cheers and applause and give him an enthusiastic send-off.

SCENE 8

While the previous scene was concerned with themes of the future and of peace, this brief scene is rooted in the present and in the Nazi preparedness for war. Hitler, Goering, and other military officials are grouped on a platform to review the infantry and cavalry and to watch a demonstration of armored vehicles and artillery participating in a mock battle. The music is military marches. In itself, the contrast between the soldiers mounted on horseback and those concealed in tanks provides an ironic comment on past and present military techniques. The soldiers in the crowd seem to enjoy the event as much as their leaders, and the scene offers a rare glimpse of Hitler laughing and smiling as he observes the brisk, spirited display.

The scene is short because of the inclement weather on the day that it was filmed, and not apparently from any desire of Riefenstahl to overlook the German Army; but, as noted previously, she was compelled to make the short film *Tag der Freiheit—Unsere Wehrmacht* to appease offended Army generals. The later film provides a much better picture of Nazi military strength than this eighth scene of *Triumph of the Will*.

SCENE 9

Here Leni Riefenstahl returns to the main theme of her film: the deification of Adolf Hitler. Photographed at a vast outdoor rally held in the early evening, the scene begins with a new stage of development. In a vast assembly attended by 180,000 party members and 250,000 spectators, only Hitler seems an individual; the men are obscured by the flags they carry. The 21,000 party standards represent 700,000 party functionaries all over Germany. The stage and the podium are constructed to place Hitler apart from his immediate entourage and, more important, high above the crowd. Here the people are reduced to architectural patterns, deprived of their individuality in favor of some larger communal ideal. This is accomplished through the use of flags, as if they were costumes, to cover the participants and through the distorted visual effects created by a telephoto lens. This reduction of people into masses is juxtaposed to an equally distorted elevation of the *Führer,* and recalls Fritz Lang's *Metropolis* (1926), reportedly one of Hitler's favorite films. From this point on, Riefenstahl continues to develop the godlike presence that began with motif and music in the early moments of the film. Now the controlling images are the recurrent shots of the huge architectural eagle and swastika and, of course, the forest of flags. Now while the canvas is crowded to the borders with men, we are given a clear picture of only one of them; the rest are supporting characters, faceless and unidentified.

Standing behind and away from the microphones on a high platform, with hands folded in front of him, Hitler addresses the assembled crowd.

> HITLER: One year ago, we met for the first time on this field; it was the first general congress of the political leaders of the National Socialist Party. [Note: The 1934 rally was the sixth party congress, but the 1933 rally, the one to which Hitler has just referred, was the first after the Nazi party gained control of Germany in January 1933.] Now, 200,000 men have assembled here, summoned by nothing but the order of their heart, nothing but the command of their fidelity. It is our people's great misery that moved us, united us in battle, and made us fight and get strong, and all those who have not suffered the same misery among their own people are therefore unable to understand us. To them it is puzzling and incomprehensible that this congress would bring hundreds of thousands together and make them bear misery, suffering, and privation. They think that such a

thing is possible only at the command of the state. They are mistaken. It is not the state that commands us, but we that command the state. It is not the state that has created us, but we that are creating the state for ourselves. This movement— it is alive, rests on rock-firm foundations, and, as long as one of us can still breathe, he will devote his strengths to this movement, and defend it, just as in the years gone by. Then drum will join drum, banner will join banner, group will join group, district will join district, and then, at last, the formerly divided people will follow this gigantic column of a united nation. It would be a crime if we ever gave up what had to be fought for and won with so much labor, sorrow, sacrifice, and distress. One cannot be disloyal to something that has given content, meaning, and purpose to one's whole life. All this would not be possible were it not directed by a great command. No human master has given us this command but the lord who has created our nation. Therefore, let us take a vow this evening, namely, at every hour, on each day, to think only of Germany, the nation, the Reich, and our German people. To our German nation—*Sieg Heil! Sieg Heil! Sieg Heil!*

Moving from its position on tracks below and to the side of the high podium, the camera records Hitler's speech in a series of shots looking up at him, shots from behind, and close-ups, medium and long shots. These shots of Hitler are intercut with shots of the faces of the listening audience of flag bearers; indeed, it is in these brief shots that we realize that there are actual men alive in that forest of flags. The architectural setting is severe, and the crowd seems lost in its vastness and in the murky haze which comes from the smoking torches. Although there are some 200,000 men marching in the stadium, we are aware of them only as a mass, not as individuals. At times the screen seems dark except for the spotlights on the eagle, the swastika, and Hitler, but it is only the mass of people that makes it seem dark.

Overall, it is a memorable scene. Maintaining the consistent growth of her principal theme, Riefenstahl has now advanced Hitler to yet a higher level. In his speech, he makes reference to the "lord who has created our nation"; through the theater and film of this spectacle, he has become that lord of creation. Now the early sequences of the film assume an added significance; here, Riefenstahl suggests that the *Führer* is the lord, that he has descended to walk among his people, to bring them food, and to receive their vows. He gives life to the individual German and to the whole state in an ever-expanding sense of wholeness.

While the camera coverage of Hitler is intimate in recording his rare smiles and nervous, eccentric manner of speech, the close-ups fail to reveal the individual man behind the official visage. Hitler is the *Führer,* the leader or guide. Implacable, stern, forbidding, he accomplishes what no leader has ever done before him; in the presence of the camera, he presents his own image and creates his own portrait. The cameras record a variety of Hitler's moods, from somber seriousness to what might even be called casual charm, but they enclose the figure within the cinematic frame of a state portrait. Hitler was short and unimpressive in stature, so speakers' platforms were constructed to make him appear taller than he actually was. In the film, we rarely see his full figure; instead, we see him from the waist up, behind podiums, sitting or standing in cars, or surrounded by people. Cameras were almost always placed below and to the front of him, looking up to him. In actuality, Hitler did not have many duties at the rally. He arrived by plane, observed the events, and spoke to his supporters. With music, motif, and movement, Riefenstahl creates the impression that he descended from an ethereal height, delivered sacred words, and infused the people with his spirit. The title of the film was the theme of the rally; Hitler chose it to underscore the triumph of his will over diverse party factions. The cine-mythical apotheosis of Adolf Hitler is nearing completion.

SCENE 10

No scene in *Triumph of the Will* is more impressive than this outdoor memorial service and military review in the vast Luitpold Arena, yet the lasting impression derives from the awesome size of the massed forces rather than from any cinematic technique or from any aspect of the director's vision. The dramatic handling of previous aspects of the film has established the figure and symbol of Hitler; for the most part, this has been done within a relatively limited camera frame, the cinematic equivalent of a portrait frame. The leader has been raised above his men, and the men have been raised above the boys, and all of them have been raised above the peasants, workers, and women; and now that night has become day, the film proceeds to show the immense strength at Hitler's command, a strength summoned by his will, as the recent purge of the SA would so clearly remind any participant. The scene is a massive demonstration of the living strength of the Nazi party, yet it begins with a tribute to the dead. Here, the *Führer*, the "lord of creation," is bringing dead Germany back to life, and here, at his hand, is the largest display of that life—almost one million men marching as if they were one single force.

The sequence opens with a panoramic view of hundreds of thousands of uniformed soldiers grouped together like so many black squares on a white field. Their groups are separated by a wide, empty road which cuts across the field from one side to the other; at one end is the platform, at the other is a war memorial. Three distant figures—Hitler, Himmler, and Lutze—are walking down the road, away from the camera and toward the cenotaph. The presence of Himmler and Lutze, respectively leaders of the SS and SA, signifies, at least for the purposes of propaganda, the theme of party unity. When Hitler came to power in March 1933, he was convinced that existing party disunity was a threat to the organization of the Nazi strength and to his authority as leader. He believed that a coup by the SA leaders was imminent, and on June 30, 1934, he ordered a purge of the SA in which SA Chief Ernst Röhm and about a thousand of his men were trapped and murdered; this so-called "night of the long knives" forms a dramatic turning point in Luchino Visconti's film *The Damned* (1969). The purge reduced the ranks and the importance of the brown-shirted SA *(Sturmab-teilung)* and placed them directly under Hitler's control. At the same time, it resulted in the elevation of the black-shirted SS *(Schutz-staffel)* under the control of Heinrich Himmler. During the party meeting, Hitler ingenuously alluded to this internecine conflict and massacre as the "black shadow" which had spread over the Nazi movement, but in a blatant lie he disassociated himself and the party from what he terms the "sin" against the SA, and absolved the SS and the remaining SA of any blame. For this reason, Himmler and Lutze and their troops were very much on display at the 1934 meeting and in the film which records it.

Riefenstahl's original intention in this sequence was to follow Hitler, Himmler, and Lutze with a camera mounted on a small car, but she complains that she "lost one of the most beautiful shots" when the SA cleared the roadway and forbade the use of the car. While disappointed, she captured some of the most memorable footage in the film from her own camera mounted in an elevator which moves on one of the towering masts which hold the ori-flammes behind the speaker's platform. For many viewers, this scene is the most memorable part of the film.

Here the solemnity and simplicity of the ceremony are matched by the dignity and restraint of the photography and editing. Beyond its visual power, though, the action is essentially static, so Riefenstahl uses the moving camera dramatically as before. Facing the approaching figure from behind the war memorial—a simple, dignified structure—the camera tracks horizontally from the right to the left, while, at the same time, the three figures move into the foreground of the frame. There are no close-ups here, for it is the tribute—not those evoking it—that is important.

Following the wreath-laying ceremony, Hitler reviews the panorama and precision of his troops as they march toward the speaker's podium, up the steps on both sides, and around and behind it. The actual parade included 97,000 men from the SA and 11,000 members of the SS. This mass movement is recorded from many angles, including the camera mounted in the elevator. There are some twelve places in the film where it is possible to see cameras, including the one in the elevator and those manned by photographers lying down in the corners of the rostrum in this scene. As noted, the cameramen were dressed in SA uniforms, but it was not always possible to conceal their equipment. In fact, little seems to have been done to camouflage it. But the presence of the cameras helps to reinforce the "reality" of the spectacle, for if the rally had been "staged" for the cameras, no doubt more care would have been exercised to conceal them.

Thousands of flag and standard bearers carry their insignia; photographed through a telephoto lens, they create a mirage-like effect bobbing up and down in the bright, clear sunlight. Hitler stands stern and erect, often with arms clasped across his chest, as he reviews the long and impressive lines of soldiers, storm troopers, and bands. Here the variety of the photography indicates the extensive planning involved in the placement and operation of the cameras; especially effective are the ground-level shots of goose-stepping storm troopers as they march down the steps toward Hitler's platform. The rally proceeds with Lutze's introduction of Hitler.

LUTZE: My *Führer!* As we have done our duty in the past, so shall we also, in the future, wait solely for your order. And we, comrades, know only one thing: to follow the order of our *Führer* and to prove that we have remained the same. Our *Führer*—Adolf Hitler! *Sieg Heil! Sieg Heil! Sieg Heil!*

HITLER: Men of the SA and the SS. A few months ago, a black shadow spread over the movement. Neither the SA, nor any other institution of the party, has anything to do with this shadow. They are all deceived who believe that even one crack has occurred in the structure of our united movement. It stands firm just as this formation here, as we in Germany stand—unbroken. And if anyone sins against the spirit of my SA, this will not break the SA but only those who dare to sin against them. Only a lunatic or a deliberate liar could think that I, or anybody, would ever intend to dissolve what we ourselves have built up over many long years. No, comrades, we are firmly standing by our Germany, and we have to stand firmly by her. I now give you the new flags, convinced that I am handing them over to the most faithful hands in Germany. In the past, you have proved your loyalty to me a thousandfold, and it cannot and will not be different in the future. And so I greet you, as my old, faithful men of the SA and SS. *Sieg Heil! Sieg Heil! Sieg Heil!*

This speech is followed by a solemn consecration of the battle flags. Hitler is on the field, moving along a line of flag-bearing troops, clutching his personal banner (his "blood flag") in his left hand while grasping the corners of their banners in his right. The flags are so thickly placed together that one barely sees, if at all, the men holding them. The effect is impressive, and suggests that Hitler is blessing each and every flag, and its bearer, with his own personal banner. The confrontation between him and each man is very personal, very direct; the eye-to-eye contact seems to single out each man as if he were the only one in the vast stadium. To give added significance, Riefenstahl breaks the spiritual nature of the flag consecration with intercut shots of cannons being fired in tribute.

Riefenstahl controls this sequence with consummate artistry, juxtaposing the dead with the living, the past with the present, the men with their leader, and finally, the spiritual with the material. The flags are consecrated with the leader's personal touch, while the booming cannons remind us both of the dead and of the military strength of the living Nazi power. In the beginning, Hitler emerged as if from the clouds, so now he moves among his men as if he were a god. Riefenstahl has created an apotheosis—and the reverse of it, too—for Hitler has come down to his people as the living embodiment of their beliefs.

In Riefenstahl's mythic conception, Hitler resembles a Christ figure, and in this second visit to Nuremberg since assuming power, a "second coming," he brings food (an action parallel to Christ's turning water into wine), he raises the dead (Christ and Lazarus), he drives the moneychangers from the temple (the purge of the dissident SA men), and he delivers a sermon from the mount (the last major speech in which the "dark shadow" is contrasted to the remaining faithful forces, the metaphorical "light" of his world). In her adaptation of German myth, Riefenstahl shows that Hitler is a political hero to his people, and by appealing to the viewer's familiarity with German myth and music, she further suggests that he is a culture hero. The central German myth is the *Nibelungenlied* (Song of the Nibelungs); following Richard Wagner's *Der Ring des Nibelungen,* the monumental cycle of four operas based on the myth, Fritz Lang made the two-part silent film *Die Nibelungen* (1923, *Siegfried,* part one, and *Kriemhild's Revenge,* part two). Lang's influence can be seen in *Triumph of the Will,* especially in Riefenstahl's epic tableaux and, to a lesser extent, in the grand architectural scale. The architectural and decorative style of Lang's studio-made film is rich in art deco design, while Albert Speer's designs for Nuremberg are simple, the primary decorative motif being the flags. Hitler identified with the Nibelungen's irrational, violent, mystical world; he adapted some of the mysticism of that primitive, demonic world to his own creation, the Nazi Third Reich.

The film does not end on this mythic note, as artistic structure and symbolism might suggest. The source of the party strength is embodied in Hitler's will and gestures and symbols are effective in conveying that strength, but the true source of Nazi power lies in the artillery and the troops. For propaganda purposes, it is that strength which must be paraded before the public and the film audience. The firm has characterized Hitler as the Nazi spiritual leader; all that remains is to chronicle the physical measure of that strength.

SCENE 11

The long parade scene shows the variety, strength, and support of German military and labor service forces from all regions of the country. A great variety of photography records the troop parade, including views from the air, from windows and apertures in buildings, from bridges, and from moving vehicles. The camera is always moving, even though the subject is, for the most part, moving also. The spirit of the scene is maintained by the lively march music. The editing shapes the lengthy footage into a structured but rhythmical montage which saves the scene from being just a tedious record of a military review. The troops and bands are photographed from many angles, so that we do not see one group from one angle and then another group from a similar camera angle. The editing keeps the angle of vision moving from one vantage point to another, accomplishing what everyone hopes for at a parade: to be everywhere at once. While the sequence in all its variety is concerned with Hitler's review of the troops, there are occasional close-ups of other party leaders, of sidewalk crowds, and notably of women. Perhaps this provides another characteristic Riefenstahl contrast—in this case, men who march and women who stand along the sidelines and watch. The rhythm of the parade is not unlike that of other parades, but Riefenstahl builds her montage to give it an almost indescribable sense of anticipation and excitement. Because she was so busy completing other sections of the film, she originally assigned the editing of this section to someone else, but she says she had to reject his work because it had the static quality of the newsreel approach she was trying to avoid.

In the Russian tradition of Eisenstein and Pudovkin and in the German adaptation of that tradition by Ruttmann, *Triumph of the Will* demonstrates the power of the rhythmic montage to provide multi-leveled impressions of each scene, no matter how minor. This retains the viewer's attention; moreover, it creates the excitement and anticipation which give the film its essence. Furthermore, this montage is appropriate editing for propaganda films because it forces the viewer to see and to feel exactly what the director wishes. No single scene in the film exemplifies this better than this lengthy parade of German military forces. One seldom grows weary in watching this longest scene in the film, which could have been its most boring, because the camera is everywhere, from the gutters to the rooftops, giving the viewer an exceptional experience. Such variety is not presented merely for its own sake, nor is it just a photographic *tour de force*. With a continuum of brief shots, basic motifs, and progressive rhythm, Riefenstahl takes the viewer *to* the events, but she also makes him a participant *in* them. The circular and symbolic structure of the film gradually becomes apparent after repeated viewings, but the immediate effect is to immerse the viewer in the dynamic reality of the events it records.

Thematically, the parade sequence confirms the idea that Germany is a massed, marching column of men. Cinematically, the montage cuts the uninterrupted wholeness of the parade into pieces and then reassembles them to produce an even larger concept of wholeness. The space and the subject are fixed—a single roadway and a parade of men; Riefenstahl manipulates and redeems that prosaic space and subject with the omniscience of multiple camera positions and the dynamics of her editing. In sequence after sequence, the troops march past the *Führer;* anticipation builds, not to relief, but only to more anticipation. Rank after rank, troop after troop, regiment after regiment, band after band—an almost endless parade of military strength. Here, as in the diving sequence of *Olympia,* Riefenstahl transcends the finite limitations of time and space and explores the infinite suggestiveness of cinematic space and form.

With arms crossed on his chest, Hitler watches the precise troops of soldiers, laborers, and motorized forces; he salutes the leaders and, from time to time, the people sitting in bleachers behind him rise from their seats to salute. Just to the left of the reviewing area is a multiple camera position, and the viewer with a quick eye will see Riefenstahl, dressed in a black sweater and a long white skirt, standing in front of it, directing the work of her cameramen.

The music begins with themes from *Die Meistersinger von Nürnberg* and continues with the sound of trumpet fanfares, cheering crowds, and military march music. Herbert Windt adds studio-recorded march music to actual sound to enhance and sustain the vitality of the varied photography and dynamic editing, which intercuts shots of the parade with shots of the crowds and of a family looking through a window. As in the opening scene, Riefenstahl varies this action with many shots of the medieval buildings. Near the end of the sequence, the pace of the marching and the music slows down; in a long shot, the camera pans across the rooftops and gives a final view of the city. This seems to be the final event for the majority of men—to pass in review before their leaders—as they march out of the city.

Between the end of the previous scene and the end of this one, the focus of the film has shifted from Hitler, as spiritual leader, to Hitler as head of the military forces. It is a natural transition, but nonetheless Hitler remains apart from all but high party officials and close aides. He reviews the parade standing alone in an open car at the curb and is separated from the crowd behind him by a great empty space. In the final scene, Riefenstahl returns to focus on Hitler as party leader; but the last scene is really the penultimate— or next to last—element in the structure of the film, for it leads us not to the conclusion but back to the beginning. Moreover, it provides a vital insight into the dynamic theory of personality on which the film is based.

SCENE 12

The closing scene of the film is the final congress of the 1934 party rally. At one end of the crowded Luitpold Hall, the large illuminated eagle dominates the platform; the platform itself is decorated with flags, banners, swastikas, and the speaker's podium is flanked by large floral displays. At the other end, the hall is dominated by a sign reading *"Alles für Deutschland"* (Everything for Germany). From a camera position above and behind the main aisle, we see Hitler enter the hall with Hess and an entourage of party officials; Hitler is smiling, but perspiring and appears to be somewhat uneasy in contrast to his comparatively calm manner at previous gatherings. They move quickly to their places on the platform, and the crowd welcomes them with a shout of *"Heil!"* The music is the *"Badenweiler Marsch,"* Hitler's favorite march, played at all his official entrances and exits. The band plays another march to accompany the standard bearers as they enter the hall up the same main aisle which separates the crowd into two sections. Hess introduces Hitler.

HESS: The *Führer* speaks!

HITLER: The sixth party congress of the movement is coming to its close. What millions of Germans outside our party ranks may have considered only a most impressive display of political power, has meant immeasurably more for the old fighters: the great personal and spiritual meeting of old fighters and comrades-in-arms. And perhaps one or the other among you, in spite of the compelling grandeur of this troop review of our party, was wistfully recalling those days when it was still difficult to be a National Socialist.

Even when our party had only seven men, it already voiced two principles: first, it wanted to be a true ideologically conditioned movement; and, second, it wanted, therefore, to be, without compromise, the sole power and the only power in Germany. As a party, we had to remain a minority because we had mobilized the most valuable elements of fighting and sacrifice in the nation, which, at all times, have amounted not to a majority, but to a minority. And because these men, the best of the German race, in proud self-confidence, have courageously and boldly claimed the leadership of this Reich and nation, the people in ever greater numbers have joined this leadership and subordinated themselves.

The German people is happy in the knowledge that the constantly changing leadership has now finally been replaced by a stabilizing force, a man who considers himself representative of the best blood, and, knowing this, has elevated himself to the leadership of this nation and is determined to keep this leadership, to use it to the best advantage, and never to relinquish it. It will always be only a part of the nation which will consist of really active fighters, and more will be asked of them than of the millions of other fellow countrymen. For them, the mere pledge 'I believe' is not enough; instead, they will swear to the oath 'I will fight!'

The party will for all time to come represent the elite of the political leadership of the German people. It will be unchangeable in its doctrine, hard as steel in its organization, supple and adaptable in its tactics; in its entity, however, it will be like a religious order. But the goal must be that all respectable Germans will become National Socialists. Only the best National Socialists are fellow members of the party.

In the past, our adversaries, through suppression and persecution, have cleaned the party from time to time of the rubbish that began to appear. Today, we ourselves must do the mustering out and the discarding of what has proven to be bad and, therefore, inwardly alien to us. It is our wish and will that this state and this Reich shall endure in the milleniums to come. We can be happy in the knowledge that this future belongs to us completely. While the older generation could still waver, the young generation has pledged itself to us and is ours, body and soul. Only when we in the party, with the cooperation of everybody, make it the highest embodiment of National Socialist thought and spirit will the party be an eternal and indestructible pillar of the German people and of our Reich. Then, eventually, the magnificent, glorious army—those old, proud warriors of our nation—will be joined by the political leadership of the party—equally tradition-minded—and then these two institutions together will educate and strengthen the German man, and carry on their shoulders the German state, the German Reich.

At this hour, tens of thousands of party members are already leaving the city. And while some of them are still revelling in remembrances, others are already beginning to prepare the next meeting—and again people will come and go, will be moved anew, be pleased and inspired, because the idea and the movement are a living expression of our nation, and, therefore, a symbol of eternity.

Long live the National Socialist movement! Long live Germany!

The text and delivery of this speech give Hitler the opportunity to proclaim his own deity, and he exploits the opportunity with histrionic techniques ranging from waving arms, to pounding fists, to visionary stares and enraptured ranting. But Riefenstahl's close-up view is extraordinary, too, for it appears to contradict the carefully made portrait that she has been creating until now. Obviously such a contradiction does not derive from any conscious attempt on the filmmaker's part, but rather emerges from the reality of the moment itself. Instead of redeeming this reality with her cinematic style, here Riefenstahl chose to focus a close-up lens on the *Führer* and to let him, literally and visually, speak for himself. In order to emphasize the text of the speech, Riefenstahl focuses directly on the speaker and does not build any montage to give the moment extra significance. As a result, Hitler does not appear as an aloof, detached figure, or a spiritual power, or a fearful military leader; instead, he appears as an excited politician carried away with himself. Apparently responding to cues in his notes, he begins the speech with a restrained voice and serious tone; as he proceeds, his voice becomes more emotional and his body moves with the passion of his thoughts; he pounds his clenched fist on the podium, waves his hands, and jabs his arm in the air for emphasis. As he nears conclusion, his delivery seems to take precedence over his words, as he expounds his vision of Germany. It is no wonder that Chaplin found so much to lampoon in *The Great Dictator*.

This is the longest speech in the film and, by its place at the final meeting, should be the most important, yet it seems notable not for its length or content, but for its hollow phrases and empty vision. It seems remarkable that such a climactic moment should have received so little attention from either the speech writers or the filmmaker, but then none of Hitler's speeches in the film are anything more than this. Under the scrutiny of the close-up lens, Hitler does not live up to the image that the preceding film has created for him.

Riefenstahl does not dwell on this irony, but brings the film to its climax. Hess' remarks conclude the official proceedings of the sixth Nazi Party rally.

HESS: The party is Hitler, but Hitler is Germany, just as Germany is Hitler! Hitler! *Sieg Heil! Sieg Heil! Sieg Heil!*

The "Horst Wessel" song, the music with which the film began, now resumes and continues through the end of the film, first played by a band and then by a pipe organ which carries the melody alone to the end. This sequence closes with a long shot of the entire hall, followed by a medium shot of the swastika which dissolves to a close-up of the swastika which then dissolves to the final shot.

The final sequence is a return to a strong statement of unity and solidarity. From a camera angle below and slightly to the right, we see a line of men marching from the left background of the frame slightly upward and toward the right foreground. They are silhouetted against the sky, and moving slowly upward, as if in quest of the heavens from which their *Führer* was seen to descend at the beginning of the rally. Here Riefenstahl returns to complete the theme of a German renaissance by suggesting a kind of spiritual resurrection through the *Führer's* leadership. The quest appears to be a slow, tedious one, requiring discipline, hard work, and a massed effort. Led by the spirit of their *Führer,* the men begin their quest; their goal—and the propaganda message of this film—is a triumph of the will. The cumulative effect of the film suggests that they will triumph over individuality, adversity, and disunity with the strength and determination of their will. Thus, the mass is related to the leader, the quest to the goal, and, with the titles, the film is completed.

summary critique

The Paradox of Propaganda

When *Triumph of the Will* was first screened in Berlin in 1935, the audience acclaimed the film for its artistry, but other less sophisticated audiences across Germany were not accustomed to such artistic propaganda and did not appreciate it. Even though the film is now regarded as a propaganda masterpiece, the Nazis did not use it so widely as its present reputation would suggest. Nonetheless, Hitler ordered that Riefenstahl be given the National Film Prize, and Goebbels presented it to her on May 1, 1935, saying:

> This film represents an exceptional achievement in the film production of the past year. It is closely relevant to us because it reflects the present: it describes in unprecedented scenes the gripping events of our political existence. It is a filmed grand vision of our *Führer,* who is shown here for the first time on the screen in the most impressive manner. The film has successfully overcome the danger of becoming a mere propaganda feature. It has lifted up the harsh rhythm of our great epoch to eminent heights of artistic achievement. It is a monumental film, thundering with the tempo of marching columns, based on iron principles redhot with creative passion.[7]

As we have seen, Goebbels did not approve of Riefenstahl's production methods, but he was impressed by her creative genius and by her film portrait of Hitler and he extolled the artist for creating masterful cinema and powerful propaganda. Today, we too acknowledge *Triumph of the Will* as a superb example of political propaganda even as we are repelled by its vision. The film is both documentary and propaganda, and moreover it succeeds in fusing politics with art. Critics of the film, however, have paid less attention to its artistic achievement than to its politics, and it has provoked three basic critical responses. First, there are the critics whose moral and political convictions prevent them from appreciating the film; second, there are those who understand the film, and even appreciate it, in light of its mission as propaganda; and third, there are those who appreciate the formal beauty of the film in spite of its politics. And, indeed, there are some critics who might agree with all three viewpoints.

The first critical position is perhaps best exemplified by Siegfried Kracauer, whose evaluation of the film has had great influence, especially on more recent critics such as David Gunston and David Stewart Hull. One part of Kracauer's argument against *Triumph of the Will* rests on the assumption that the rally was staged for the film; while this is inaccurate, his central assertion underscores the conflict between reality and art and illuminates one's understanding of the film. Kracauer writes:

> Through a very impressive composition of mere newsreel shots, *this film represents the complete transformation of reality,* its complete absorption into the artificial structure of the Party convention [my italics] (Kracauer, 300).

While Kracauer sees the footage as "mere newsreel shots," Richard Griffith acclaims Riefenstahl for the "psychic world which she created out of nothing with camera and shears" (Rotha and Griffith, 591). Riefelstahl insists that the film is a documentary:

> The film is purely historical. I state precisely; it is *film-vérité*. It reflects the truth that was then, in 1934, history. It is therefore a documentary. Not a propaganda film. Oh! I know very

well what propaganda is. That consists of recreating certain events in order to illustrate a thesis or, in the face of certain events, to let one thing go in order to accentuate another (Delahaye, 392–93).

Both Kracauer and Riefenstahl are right, and both are wrong, to a certain extent. The party rally transformed the political reality of 1934 with a spectacular display of party unity, and the film recorded that display. To that extent, the rally was propaganda, and so the film was both documentary and propaganda, a record of reality and a transformation of reality. But it is in the transformation of reality into a heroic and inspiring vision that the film has its power.

A second critical position is occupied primarily by those who accept the necessity for propaganda filmmaking; they do not support the politics of Riefenstahl's film but they are impressed with her artistry as a propaganda filmmaker. Among such is John Grierson, the founder of the British documentary movement, who praised her film and later defended her against British attacks in the early 1960s, a defense that was later articulated in a more scholarly manner by Kevin Brownlow. Robert Flaherty, the American pioneer of documentary filmmaking, also understood the power of propaganda films and regretted that *Triumph of the Will* could not have been shown in the United States to warn people against Hitler.

A third critical position is held by those critics for whom cinematic form is more important than content; for them, a propaganda film must transform politics into art. There has been considerably less formalist criticism of *Triumph of the Will* than one might expect considering its reputation as a masterpiece of cinematic invention and energy; yet, even here, critical silence is understandable, considering the film's fascist politics. In a formalist analysis, Ken Kelman writes:

Propaganda is hardly less true than any traditional art which seeks to achieve certain specific emotional effects, to manifest a vision of the world compellingly. Its poor reputation rests largely on the fact that it succeeds so seldom or partially. Such failure is virtually a condition of the fiction propaganda film, where the world presented is not necessarily the real one, where the work is ostensibly imagined, and though emotion may be stirred, it is not stirred by the facts of life. Since propaganda is concerned with influencing attitudes toward life in a given time and place, and indeed in terms of specific events and people, its ideal must always be to present this life, these events, these people. . . .

However, *Triumph of the Will* did come to surpass *Potemkin* as the ultimate in cinema propaganda. This is for one essential reason: *Triumph* is a true documentary, completely made up of 'actual' footage—the ultimate in incontrovertible credibility. *The wonderful paradox here is that under any conditions but this absolute reportorial truth, the propaganda itself would be quite incredible* [my italics] (Kelman, 162).

Each of these three critical positions articulates an individual approach to evaluating *Triumph of the Will* and each is useful in helping one to gain a better understanding of the film, but none offers more than partial answers to the large questions posed. The film is a masterful blend of the four basic elements of cinema—light, darkness, sound, and silence—but it is not just an achievement in cinematic form, for it has other essential elements—thematic, psychological, mythological, narrative, and visual interest—and it is in the working of these elements that Riefenstahl transcends the limitations of the documentary film and the propaganda film genres.

Riefenstahl's art is to perceive the essence of a real situation and to transfer the form, content, and meaning of that essential moment to the screen. In short, she is a poet. Through her handling of myth, she extends the meaning of the immediate moment by enriching its cultural significance. In the history of world cinema, *Tri-*

umph of the Will stands as Riefenstahl's brilliant fusion of prosaic film footage with her mythic vision of reality. As such, it has not been imitated directly, nor has its footage been successfully used against it, as so often happens with propaganda and counter-propaganda films. When Luis Buñuel showed his edited version of *Triumph of the Will* to an audience consisting of President Roosevelt, René Clair, and Charles Chaplin, they all agreed that the film was too good to be used against itself.[8] For Riefenstahl, the precision marching of the Nazi troops was an objective reality, although her subjective photography and editing added a menacing power to it. For Chaplin, however, this behavior of men as if they were machines was the essence of comedy. Diffuse as it is, *The Great Dictator* (1940) appears to be a direct parody of Riefenstahl's film. It tells us the same thing about Hitler and the party, but it does it in an intentionally comic mode. In the role of the dictator Hynkel, Chaplin mercilessly caricatures Hitler's manner of walking and talking, and he illumines Riefenstahl's implicit propaganda—that the *Führer* is a god—by exposing the absurd idea for what it is. Ultimately, Chaplin tells us more about Hitler than all of Riefenstahl's brilliant montage and music possibly can, for he probes beneath the military surface to find the insanity of humans pretending to be what they cannot be.

With varying degrees of sucess, footage from *Triumph of the Will* has been used in anti-Nazi propaganda films. The best known are the seven films in Frank Capra's "Why We Fight" series. In England, the film was studied extensively and parts were used in Fred Watt's *The Curse of the Swastika* (1940), John Grierson's humorous *Germany Calling* (1940), and in the Donald Taylor and Dylan Thomas collaboration *These Are the Men* (1943). Paul Rotha made use of it in a West German film titled *The Life of Adolf Hitler* (*Das Leben Adolf Hitlers*, 1961). Parts of it are evident in the Soviet film on the Nuremberg trials, Roman Karmen's and Yelizaveta Svilova's *Trial by the Peoples* (1946 and 1962), and in Erwin Leiser's *Mein Kampf* (1960) and *Germany Awakens* (*Deutschland Erwache,* 1968). Shots and scenes from the film have been extensively used in documentaries for such television series as "The Twentieth Century" and "Project XX." In other ways, not concerned with direct influence, one cannot help remembering *Triumph of the Will* when seeing such films as Mel Brooks' *The Producers* (1968), Stanley Kramer's *Judgment at Nuremberg* (1961), Louis Clyde Stoumen's *The Black Fox* (1962), Alain Resnais' *Night and Fog* (1955), Luchino Visconti's *The Damned* (1969), and Philippe Mora's *Swastika* (1973).

Leni Riefenstahl's *Triumph of the Will* reminds us of Hitler's plans for creating a German renaissance through Nazi party unity and military strength. Unintentionally, it recalls our memories of a madman whose ideas of rebirth led to genocide. It reminds us of unspeakable evil, of the ghastly stillness that moves one now in the ruins of Dachau, Buchenwald, Mauthausen, Auschwitz, Sachsenhausen, Treblinka, and Belsen. It reminds us that man can be irrational, that people can follow false gods, and that it is all too humanly possible to make Hell seem like Heaven. The film does all of this and more, and yet it has another great power—cinematic power. The power and the paradox of *Triumph of the Will* is that it can repel us and attract us at the same time.

a Riefenstahl filmography
bibliography
rental sources
notes

a Riefenstahl filmography

This filmography includes the titles of films directed by Leni Riefenstahl (marked with an *) and those in which she appeared; for a more extensive listing, see *Film Culture* (Spring 1973) which reprints, with corrections, the filmography prepared by Riefenstahl for the German publication *Filmkritik* (August 1972).

Der Heilige Berg (The Holy Mountain), 1926

Der Grosse Sprung (The Great Leap), 1927

Das Schicksal Derer von Habsburg (The Fate of the von Hapsburgs), 1929

Die Weisse Hölle von Piz Palü (The White Hell of Pitz Palu), 1929

Stürme über dem Montblanc (Storm Over Mont Blanc), 1930 (also known as *Avalanche*)

Der Weisse Rausch (The White Frenzy), 1931

*Das Blaue Licht (The Blue Light), 1932; reissue, 1952

SOS Eisberg (S. O. S. Iceberg), 1933

*Sieg des Glaubens (Victory of Faith), 1933

*Triumph des Willens (Triumph of the Will), 1935

*Tag der Freiheit—Unsere Wehrmacht (Day of Freedom—Our Armed Forces), 1935

*Olympia: Part 1: *Fest der Völker (Festival of Nations);* Part 2: *Fest der Schönheit (Festival of Beauty)*, 1938

*Tiefland (Lowland), 1954

selected bibliography

Barsam, Richard Meran. *Nonfiction Film: A Critical History.* New York: E. P. Dutton & Co., 1973.
Critical, chronological survey of development of nonfiction film in U.S. and G.B. between 1920 and 1970.
————. "Leni Riefenstahl: Artifice and Truth in a World Apart," *Film Comment* (November–December 1973), 32–37.
Overall appraisal of director's career.

Berson, Arnold and Joseph Keller. "Shame and Glory in the Movies," *National Review,* 14 January 1964, 17–21.
Comparative analysis in conservative journal of American liberal attitudes toward Eisenstein and Riefenstahl; quotes excerpts from John Grierson's article in defense of director.

Brownlow, Kevin. "Leni Riefenstahl," *Film* (Winter 1966), 14–19.
A sensitive, persuasive defense of director, based on interview.
————. "Reply to Paul Rotha," *Film* (Spring 1967), 14–15.
Brownlow answers Rotha's attack on Riefenstahl, printed in same issue; see also Riefenstahl's reply to Rotha.

Burden, Hamilton T. *The Nuremberg Party Rallies: 1923–1939.* New York: Praeger Publishers, 1967.
Informative historical introduction; descriptions of events and programs; certain errors in comments on rally films.

Champlin, Charles. "Buñuel in Hollywood—Star Billing After 27 Years," *Los Angeles Times Calendar,* 3 December 1972, 1.
Information on Buñuel's editing of *Triumph* for short anti-Nazi version.

[Cocteau, Jean]. "Four Letters by Jean Cocteau to Leni Riefenstahl," *Film Culture* (Spring 1973), 90–93.

Letters of admiration from a fellow artist; in French, with English translation; illustrated.

Corliss, Richard. "Leni Riefenstahl: A Bibliography," *Film Heritage* (Fall 1969), 27–36.

Delahaye, Michel. "Interview with Leni Riefenstahl" in *Interviews with Film Directors,* ed. Andrew Sarris. Indianapolis: Bobbs-Merrill Co., 1967.
English translation of *Cahiers du Cinema* interview; material here complements that in Hitchens' interviews.

Everson, William K. "Triumph of the Will" in *The Documentary Tradition: From Nanook to Woodstock,* ed. Lewis Jacobs. New York: Hopkinson & Blake, 1972, 138–40.
Brief review of the film; among those few reviews available in English, notable for its objectivity.

Fuentes, Carlos. "The Discreet Charm of Luis Buñuel," *The New York Times Magazine,* 11 March 1973, 27–29ff.
Includes full account of his work in preparing short anti-Nazi propaganda version of *Triumph of the Will.*

Gardner, Robert. "Can the Will Triumph?", *Film Comment* (Winter 1965), 28–31.
Comments on director's ability to survive her critics; in issue featuring articles on director and her work.

Gunston, David. "Leni Riefenstahl," *Film Quarterly* (Fall 1960), 4–19.
One of the first, and the longest article on director in an American film journal; now outdated, but nonetheless useful.

Hitchens, Gordon. "An Interview with a Legend," *Film Comment* (Winter 1965), 6–11.
First interview in English; still excellent source of information.

———. "Henry Jaworsky, Cameraman for Leni Riefenstahl, Interviewed by Gordon Hitchens, Kirk Bond, and John Hanhardt," *Film Culture* (Spring 1973), 122–61.

Valuable, new information on 1930s German filmmaking and on working with Riefenstahl on *Olympia*.

————. "Leni Riefenstahl Interviewed by Gordon Hitchens," *Film Culture* (Spring 1973), 94–121.

Second Hitchens interview contains especially valuable information about her activities after second world war.

Hull, David Stewart. *Film in the Third Reich*. Berkeley, California: University of California Press, 1969.

Presently the only comprehensive study of the subject in English.

Kelman, Ken. "Propaganda as Vision: *Triumph of the Will*," *Film Culture* (Spring 1973), 162–66.

Discussion of cinematic form as propaganda.

Kracauer, Siegfried. *From Caligari to Hitler: A Psychological History of the German Film*. Princeton, New Jersey: Princeton University Press, 1947.

Unique "psychological history" of German film leaves much unsaid; provocative, influential discussion of Riefenstahl.

Leiser, Erwin. "La Vérité sur Leni Riefenstahl et 'Le Triomphe de la Volonté'," *Cinema 69* (February 1969), 72–78.

Discussion of legal questions surrounding use of *Triumph* footage in his and others' compilation films; heavily biased and generally unreliable on legal facts; written by one of Riefenstahl's most outspoken critics; in French.

Manvell, Roger and Heinrich Fraenkel. *The German Cinema*. New York: Praeger Publishers, 1971.

Chapters 4 and 5 give a succinct history of filmmaking in Nazi Germany; complements Hull's study.

Richards, Jeffrey. "Leni Riefenstahl: Style and Structure," *The Silent Picture* (Autumn 1970), 17–19.
Discusses influence of German silent tradition on Riefenstahl; in English film journal.

Riefenstahl, Leni. *Hinter den Kulissen des Reichsparteitagfilms.* Munich: Zentralverlag der NDSAP, Franz Eher Nachf., 1935.
Promotion booklet for *Triumph* gives valuable "behind the scenes" information on production; however, text is mainly propaganda in its praise of party and film; actually written by Ernst Jäger; in German.

―――. *Kampf im Schnee und Eis.* Leipzig: Hesse and Becker Verlag, 1933.
Personal account of learning to ski, climb, and make mountain films; in German.

―――. *The Last of the Nuba.* New York: Harper and Row, 1974.
Pictorial and anthropological study of African tribe.

―――. "Reply to Paul Rotha," *Film* (Spring 1967), 15.
Defends herself against Rotha's attack; see Brownlow's defense in same issue.

―――. *Schönheit im Olympischen Kampf.* Berlin: Im Deutschen Verlag, 1937.
Illustrated account of *Olympia* production; in German.

―――. "Why I am Filming *Penthesilea*," *Film Culture* (Spring 1973), 192–215.
Detailed production notes for her long-unrealized film project; rare glimpse of her overall concept and preparation of a film.

Rotha, Paul. "Leni Riefenstahl," *Film* (Spring 1967), 8–12.
Answer to Brownlow's article in *Film* (Winter 1966); attacks politics of Riefenstahl's art; see replies to Rotha by Brownlow and Riefenstahl in same issue; see Grierson's remarks quoted by Berson and Keller.

Waggoner, Walter H. "British Film Group Withdraws Its Invitation to Friend of Hitler," *New York Times,* 9 January 1960, 2.

News report on action of British Film Institute which prompted Grierson's defense quoted in Berson and Keller.

Weigel, Herman. "Randbemerkungen zum Thelma," *Filmkritik* (August 1972), 426–33.

Summary, random account of Riefenstahl's careeer, in issue of German film journal on her life and work; in German.

rental sources

Triumph of The Will is available for rent from the sources listed below. The analysis in this study is based on circulating prints from the Museum of Modern Art. The Contemporary and Macmillan prints contain English subtitles which, as noted previously, are not accurate.

Circulation Director, Department of Film, Museum of Modern Art, 11 West 53rd Street, New York, New York　10019

Contemporary Films/McGraw-Hill Films, Princeton Road, Hightstown, New Jersey　08520

Macmillan Audio Brandon, 34 MacQuesten Parkway South, Mount Vernon, New York　10550

Day of Freedom—Our Armed Forces is available for rent from:

Film Images, Division of Radim Films, 1034 Lake Street, Oak Park, Illinois　60301

notes

1. All remarks by Leni Riefenstahl not documented from another source are from interviews with me held in Munich, Germany, in December 1972 and January 1973.

2. Hull (136–37) says that she made a "mysterious" film entitled *Berchtesgaden über Salzburg* (1938) about Hitler's retreat, the "Eagle's Nest," high in the mountains at Berchtesgaden, near Salzburg. Hull's information came from James Manilla, "A Review of a Lesser Riefenstahl Work," *Film Comment* (Winter 1965), 23. In a 1973 conversation with me, Mr. Manilla acknowledged his error in identifying this as a Riefenstahl film. In addition, Riefenstahl told me that she did not make such a film. From the footage included in Philippe Mora's film *Swastika* (1973), it appears that the film was made by Hitler's lover, Eva Braun.

3. Gordon Hitchens, "An Interview with a Legend," *Film Comment* (Winter 1965), 7.

4. Despite elaborate precautions, some footage was spoiled, and a setting simulating the Luitpold Hall (speaker's rostrum only) was constructed in a studio for a retake of the Streicher speech. In *Inside the Third Reich* (New York, Avon Books, 1971, 100), Albert Speer suggests a larger studio production, but Riefenstahl says that Speer does not remember correctly.

5. Leni Riefenstahl, *Hinter den Kulissen des Reichsparteitagfilms* (Munich, Zentralverlag Franz Eher Nachf., 1935). For publicity purposes, the title page lists Riefenstahl as the author, but a signed agreement, in Riefenstahl's archive, indicates that she employed Ernst Jäger, then editor of *Film-Kurier* in Berlin, to write it for her.

6. This is a line from the "Horst Wessel" song. Wessel was a young Nazi student and stormtrooper, killed in 1930, who left a march-

ing song based on familiar party melodies; the song became the official Nazi anthem. For Goebbels, Wessel was an ideal symbol of a hero who had given his life for the party. Although the melody is heard notably at the beginning and ending of the film, it is particularly relevant in this scene.

7. From the award certificate, in the Leni Riefenstahl archive.

8. Carlos Fuentes, "The Discreet Charm of Luis Buñuel," *New York Times Magazine,* 11 March 1973, 87. Buñuel's short version of the film was once available from the Museum of Modern Art, but has now been withdrawn from circulation.